How to Study the Bible

Mel is a thoughtful analyst of church life today. Best of all—he actually does what he writes about.

—John Ortberg, author and pastor

Having known Mel Lawrenz for thirty-five years in various capacities as student, intern, colleague, and eventual successor as senior pastor of Elmbrook Church, I can testify to his keen mind, his profound respect for and knowledge of history, his forward-looking curiosity, his undoubted communication gifts, and his many years as a seasoned practitioner of church ministry.

—Stuart Briscoe, author and pastor

Mel Lawrenz's vision of a local church that actually reflects the wholeness and beauty of God as it engages with the Lord, one another, and the community is a much-needed call back to God's original Plan A – a plan that has too often been cast aside in the name of specialization, church growth, and expediency.

—Larry Osborne, author and pastor

HOW TO
STUDY

THE
BIBLE

MEL LAWRENZ

WWW.WORDWAY.ORG

WordWay
How to Study the Bible
Copyright © 2019 Mel Lawrenz
This title is available as a Kindle ebook.
Requests for information should be addressed to:
WordWay Resources P.O. Box 231, Waukesha, WI 53186

Published by WordWay Resources LLC
www.wordway.org

All Scripture quotations, unless otherwise indicated, are taken from The Holy Bible, New International Version. Copyright © 1973, 1978, 1984, 2011, by Biblica, Inc.

Editing: Micah Matthews
Cover and interior design: Sheila Hahn

CONTENTS

To the Reader

It is a truly astonishing thing, when you think about it, that when you hold a Bible in your hand, you are grasping a treasury of truth and a source of life.

Grasping it in our hands is one thing, grasping it in our minds and hearts, is another. The purpose of this book is to help us toward that great purpose.

If you are a believer in Jesus Christ you are called a "disciple," which literally means *a learner*. We long to follow Jesus. To take in his life-changing truth, to imitate his life, to grow in character. That's what a disciple of Jesus desires.

To be a "learner" in the family of Christ means to be a "learner" when it comes to the word of God. Jesus himself is "the Word," and Holy Scripture, both Old and New Testaments, is called "the word of God."

So why should we be concerned about Bible study? The word *study* refers to zeal and devotion. A hunger to know and understand. A curiosity that goes deeper. A commitment to reading and interpreting the words of the biblical authors according to their true meaning.

That is the purpose of this book. The zeal that we have to know God, and to know the true meaning of the word of God is the starting point. And then there are all the methods and techniques and tools that help us do that. This book is meant to be a practical guide. You will find it simple and straightforward.

This book is for any believer, and for those who lead Bible studies, teach the Bible, or use the Bible in ministry.

You may wish to work through this book with a Bible study group. Or with a class. Or with a congregation. *How to Study the Bible: A Practical Guide* aims at helping people be students of the Bible as part of their following Jesus Christ. It builds upon a previous book, *How to Understand the Bible: A Simple Guide*, which offers an overview of the actual content of the Bible.

Many blessings to you as you walk into the goldmine of God's powerful word.

Just keep in mind that, to get to the treasure, you've got to do some digging. You will be glad you did.

Mel Lawrenz

Get free supplemental resources for
individuals and groups at:

www.WordWay.org/HowToStudyTheBible

Part I

BEING A STUDENT OF SCRIPTURE

Chapter 1

IT'S ALL ABOUT ZEAL

Presumably you are holding this book in your hands right now because you are interested in understanding, studying, and applying the Bible. If so, you have made a very important decision. The Bible is not an ordinary book. Its words are the life of God and the light of God. It is the answer to decay and darkness. It is goodness coming up strong against evil. When the prophets and apostles spoke and wrote words that they knew were inspired by God's Spirit, they were depositing into human history a knowledge of God and of all reality that would shape whole civilizations and shape us.

I read the Bible occasionally when I was growing up, but it wasn't until I was 17 years old and a friend put an easy-to-understand version of the New Testament in my hand that I experienced the ring of truth and the deliciousness of God's word. I devoured that New Testament in one summer, a summer that changed the whole trajectory of my life because from then on I knew where I could hear the voice of God enlightening me, confronting me, beckoning me, filling me, correcting me, inspiring me.

I was motivated to read the Bible—slowly, methodically, prayerfully—but I also learned about studying the Bible.

I want you to be encouraged by the rich blessings of studying the Bible, and not to be intimated by the effort that it takes. Studying the Bible is for every believer. You do not need to know Hebrew and Greek or invest a thousand dollars in books in order to study the Bible. Bible study is not just for pastors and professors.

The word *study* (from Latin *studium*) refers to devotion, concentration, and zeal. So when you pick up the Bible and read, longing to understand it and being willing to submit to it, you are studying the Bible. This holy process begins before you turn to any Bible study tool. Studying the Bible begins in the soul. It begins when you open the Bible and say to God: *I want to know you more, and I am willing to read intently, with devotion, concentration, and curiosity.* If it is true the Bible is the word of God, then studying the Bible is studying God himself. When we are in a conversation with a friend or spouse we are not just listening to understand the words, we are seeking to understand the person behind the words. Bible study, in other words, is all about knowing God.

Now, there are many things we can do to study the Bible that go beyond simply reading it. In this book, we will look into biblical book studies, character studies, thematic studies, and other methods. But it all depends on this: what is in our hearts? Do we want to hear a word from God? Do we have a sense of responsibility to do the work of discerning the true meaning of biblical texts? Will we concentrate on the Scriptures as a lifestyle, knowing that, with the passage of years, we will become better, wiser people?

This book is divided into three parts. Part I delves into *being a student of Scripture*. This part is concerned with our basic posture as we read and reflect and study. On the one hand, we need to read the Bible like we would read any book, looking for the author's intent, taking the language of Scripture at face value. On the other hand, we take a posture of faith and submission because we can only get the full meaning of Scripture when we trust what it says, and because the books of the Bible invite us, in different ways, to have faith in God and deepen our faith in God. We need to foster our curiosity and develop our powers of observation. Curiosity energizes us to do the work of digging deep, and careful observation allows us to understand the fullness of the biblical text by noticing all the small, revealing details.

In Part II, we look at *ways of studying the Bible*. This is methodology. How do we approach a biblical book, understanding the flow of meaning in it? How do we study a particular passage? How do we unpack the meaning of words, and how do we develop our biblical vocabulary so that, in the natural reading of Scripture, we can draw on our accumulated Bible knowledge? How can we chase down a specific topic in Scripture, or study a particular character? How should we use basic tools like Bible dictionaries and commentaries?

Finally, in Part III, we look at *interpreting and applying the Bible*. The whole point of studying the Bible is to discover the real, objective meaning of the text. That is where the life is. That is where the power and the truth are to be found. When people make the Bible say what they want it to say, it is not only dishonest and powerless, but it is disrespectful to God. None of us like to have words put in our mouths—we might wonder what God thinks about having words put in his mouth. In Part III we also look at the dynamic of illumination and the process of right application. We consider how the truth of God's word can be planted deeply in us and how we can digest and assimilate Scripture. We also look at how to recognize false teaching.

When it comes to studying the Bible, we are in this together. We may read the Bible privately, in the quiet early morning hours or in a solitary place, but all Scripture was written for the community of faith. Each believer is a student of Scripture, but it is as we study the Bible together that we gain the full insights and blessings it offers.

Chapter 2

WHICH BIBLE?

The first question we must answer when studying the Bible is, "Which Bible?" Every student of the Bible is going to decide, first of all, which translation or translations to use. But there is a prior issue: how much of the Bible? And the answer must be, the whole Bible.

That may seem obvious, but it's easy for us to focus on the New Testament, or on other subsections of Scripture we are attracted to. Some people really like the Gospels. Others feel most at home in the letters of the apostle Paul. Some are attracted to the poetry of the Bible, or the historical narratives, or the prophecies. But we risk misinterpretation and skewing of the meaning of the text if we do not study the totality of what the prophets and apostles taught, and in balance.

Commenting on Paul's statement in Acts 20:27, "I did not shrink from declaring to you the whole counsel of God," New Testament scholar D. A. Carson says Paul "taught the burden of the whole of God's revelation, the balance of things, leaving nothing out that was of primary importance, never ducking the hard bits, helping believers to grasp the whole counsel of God that they themselves would become better equipped to read their Bibles intelligently, comprehensively" (*Preach the Word*, Crossway, 2007).

There are times when our study of the Bible will focus on specific books and passages, but we need to continually scan the whole of the Bible. We must see both the forest and the trees. There are many good Bible reading plans that structure reading through all of Scripture in a year. For a faster overview, there are 90-day Bible reading plans that help us grasp the whole scope of Scripture within a tight timeframe.

What about translations? Why are there so many options? Is there one "correct" translation?

Rendering the meaning of the original biblical texts from Hebrew, Aramaic, and Greek into the language we use is a dynamic process. There are various translations of the Bible because language changes, and because different translators have specific purposes. The English we use today has changed from the English 500 years ago, for instance. Many Bible readers can compensate for that (by becoming experts, really, in older forms of English), but others prefer a modern translation that uses today's language. (Translators refer to this as the "receptor language.")

What are sometimes called "word-for-word" translations have the advantage of showing the reader the specific word choice and phraseology of the biblical authors. Another approach is to go "thought-for-thought." These versions are true to the biblical author if they authentically render the intended meaning. Paraphrases often render whole sentences in new ways. These versions benefit people who are looking to catch the whole flow of Scripture, not so much the verse-by-verse meaning.

The debates over Bible translations can be intense because the Bible is important to us—which is a good thing! But we all should recognize that the most important thing is that we actually *read* the Bible. The best translation is the one that you will be able to read and understand in a natural way. If you are serious about studying the Bible you will look to several versions. One of the basic skills of studying the Bible is to read and compare different translations. We'll get to that later.

Here is a list of the most widely sold Bibles (in English) today, and some of the best study Bibles.

English Standard Version—an "essentially literal" update of the widely used Revised Standard Version.

New International Version — a standard translation using universally used English (thus, "International").

New Living Translation—an easy-to-read thought-by-thought translation from Hebrew and Greek.

King James Version—the classic 1611 translation. A landmark in English literature, but far removed from contemporary English.

New King James Version—a very literal translation, updating the language of the King James Version.

Common English Bible—a translation blending word-for-word and thought-for-thought approaches.

New American Standard Bible—widely seen as the most literal translation produced in the 20th century.

The Message—a free translation by Eugene Peterson using everyday modern English, idea for idea.

Two of the most helpful study Bibles are The NIV Study Bible (Zondervan) and The ESV Study Bible (Crossway).

To study the Bible is to study God (remember that the word *study* refers to devotion, concentration, and zeal). We need to have a zeal to grow in our comprehension of all parts of Scripture. In the same way that we can only understand our spouses or children or friends by understanding them as whole people, we will study Scripture best when we are peering intently at the whole.

Chapter 3

HOW SCRIPTURE EXAMINES US

I had left a large evangelistic rally in our city, Milwaukee, one day when I was 21 years old, and was surprised to see the speaker, Leighton Ford, walking across the parking lot where I happened to be. Seeing an opportunity to talk to the great man, I introduced myself and told him I was going to seminary the following year because I believed I was called to be a pastor. Ford stood several inches taller than me, and had piercing but kind eyes. I will never forget what happened next. He took his large black Bible and held it over my head. He said, "Listen, when you're in seminary you are going to be studying the Scriptures. But always remember this: you must never place yourself over Scripture. You must always place yourself under its truth and authority." That thought and that image remained with me virtually every day for the next three years while I was in seminary, and during many years of ministry afterward.

We do a lot of reading. We read news articles, editorials, stories, advice columns, blog posts, and tweets. Most of our non-fiction reading is done in order to solve a problem. How to fix a toilet. What vitamins to take. What sights to see at a vacation destination. We read to get information, and that influences our relationship with what we read. We evaluate it, deciding whether or not to believe it. We use the information for our practical needs and then forget it, because there are limits to how much we can remember.

Many people study the Bible exactly that way, looking for information, solving a problem, seeking a certain emotional effect. But if the very reason the Bible exists is because the Creator of the universe spoke through prophets and apostles to establish and deepen our relationship with him, then how we read Scripture must be different. We read it not merely for information, but for formation. We examine Scripture while it examines us.

Think about this for a moment: what have been the most formative spiritual experiences in your life—formative in the sense that they shaped you by opening your mind to a large truth, or by softening your heart, or by instilling values, or by confronting your sin? Reading Scripture ought to be one of those experiences.

We may not be aware of it every day, but over a long period of time we are formed and transformed by the truth of God.

This will not happen if we stand over the Bible as though we were masters of the text.

In his book, *Shaped by the Word*, Robert Mulholland describes formational reading in these ways:

• Formational reading is not concerned with quantity.

• Informational reading is linear; formational reading is in depth.

• Informational reading's task is to master the text; formational reading's purpose is for the text to master you.

• With formational reading "instead of the text being an object we control... the text becomes the subject of the reading relationship; we are the object that is shaped by the text."

• "Instead of the analytical, critical, judgmental approach of informational reading, formational reading requires a humble, detached, willing, loving approach."

• Informational reading is problem solving; formational reading is openness to mystery.

The 18th century scholar Johann Albrecht Bengel put it this way: "Apply yourself wholly to the text; apply the text wholly to yourself."

It is easy for us to give a head nod to this idea, to think that we know about letting Scripture shape us. But this requires diligence. In the busyness of life we may read Scripture quickly and superficially. We may read with the attitude, *what's in it for me?* Worst of all, we sometimes read in order to feel righteous.

This is why prayer must go hand in hand with studying Scripture. We talk to God, then God talks to us, then we talk to God again. And so it goes. Along the way we use Bible study techniques (which we'll get to in later chapters), but the attitude must be consistent. Whether we are studying a biblical character or an era of history or the background of a particular book or a theological truth, the work is always about knowing God and letting his word examine us.

James puts it well when he says, "Do not merely listen to the word, and so deceive yourselves. Do what it says. Anyone who listens to the word but does not do what it says is like someone who looks at his face in a mirror and, after looking at himself, goes away and immediately forgets what he looks like. But whoever looks intently into the perfect law that gives freedom, and continues in it—not forgetting what they have heard, but doing it—they will be blessed in what they do" (James 1:22-25).

In one simple statement James demolishes all superficial forms of Bible study. All of us have had days when we do Bible reading or study as a mechanical, obligatory action. We do it in order to check it off our "to do" list.

James says, no, we cannot give Scripture a quick glance and then walk away. We must "continue in it." We must apply its meaning at the first possible opportunity, otherwise we will simply forget the truths we find. And so we must "look intently into the perfect law," not in order to be slavishly and mindlessly compliant, but to move into the freedom that comes from an engaging relationship with God.

As we study Scripture, it is examining us. We need its honesty, its discernment, and its power.

Chapter 4

FACTS AND FAITH

Before we talk about the methods of studying the Bible, we need to consider our purposes. This is not a theoretical question. It is about checking our motives and shaping our attitudes before we enter into the spectacular and challenging task of hearing the voice of the living God.

One can approach Bible study as a search for facts. Who wrote this passage? Where was the author writing from, and to whom, and for what purpose? When was this written? What is the exact meaning of the language used?

We look at history, geography, culture, and language. We need to do this because the only way to thoroughly understand the texts of the Bible is to pay careful attention to the content and circumstances of the texts. Here is where curiosity goes a long way. If we think of history, geography, culture, and language as meaningful and interesting, our curiosity will draw us in to the gold in the goldmine.

This is a matter of respect. When I get a letter in the mail, I first look at the return address to see who wrote to me. I can look at the date it was posted and, by the postmark, see where it was mailed from. Then I open the letter and read the contents. If it is a handwritten letter from my mother I will read it carefully and respectfully. If it is a bill, I will read it carefully as well (but with less enthusiasm).

I do not go to the mailbox, open a letter, and just start reading, wondering how the words will impress me, or if they will make me happy. We must not read Scripture that way either. We read it respecting the author and the context. We follow the rules that apply to the use of ordinary language because God's word comes to us in the diverse and amazing forms of poems and songs, oracles and proverbs, similes and metaphors, gospels and epistles. We read Scripture naturally.

We read a passage *in context* because that is the way we see its meaning. In the same way that we hope people will take the words we use in speech or writing in context so that they will truly understand what we intend to say, we read the biblical authors in context in order to get the true meaning. This is to respect them.

And it is to respect God.

That is the other side of the equation. We read Scripture seeking to understand the facts, but we do not stop there. We read Scripture with faith. Many people, of course, are not interested in a faith journey. They are only looking at the facts. Not everyone who studies the Bible believes he or she is listening for the voice of God, and that makes all the difference in the world. It is possible to study the Bible as a purely academic exercise, and many people do. In their view, the texts in the Hebrew, Aramaic, and Greek portions of the Bible are no different from any other ancient texts. (Although many have started to read the Bible with no faith, and have been startled by the light of truth that awakened them to the reality of God.)

We read the Bible with faith, not just as informational reading. We can and must read Scripture on a factual basis of objective reality, but with the aim to know God better, which is the aim of faith.

Anselm of Canterbury (c. 1033-1109) said, "I believe in order that I may understand" (*Credo ut intelligam*). The principle is otherwise known as "faith seeking understanding," as it was expressed by Augustine of Hippo in the fourth century.

These leading thinkers—and many others—have said it is when our lives are connected with our Creator, when our minds and hearts are awakened to his power and presence, when we are "believers," that we will begin to understand the way things really are.

Knowing the Bible is not the ultimate objective. Knowing God is the ultimate objective. Really knowing God. And knowing God through the revelation God has given of himself, not our imaginary constructs. Studying Scripture in this way is about both facts and faith.

One last point here. Skeptics will say that taking a faith approach to the Bible contradicts a factual approach. That one either examines the Bible with all the tools of literary analysis and cultural criticism, or takes a religious perspective. That is not true. We can study the Bible in detail with all the typical tools of analysis of language and history, come to the conclusion that we believe what it says, and then continue to take both approaches for the rest of our lives. To say we believe that Jesus really did rise from the dead, a supernatural event, does not mean we cease to examine the text of Scripture with the canons of deductive logic. Approaching Scripture as a matter of facts and faith gives us the advantage of discovering true, objective meaning, and deepening our relationship with God.

Chapter 5

OBSERVATION

M any people love detective stories, and probably for different reasons. It's not the chase scenes or the gunfights or the big finales I enjoy; the stories I appreciate feature detectives who use their acute observational powers to discover the truth of a situation. Detectives who see details no one else sees, who make connections and understand inferences. Sherlock Holmes is at his best when he sees what few others see, piecing together clues, finding a larger truth. I come away from such stories wishing I had that kind of sharp eye—the ability to see things the way they really are in all of life.

We begin our study of the Bible with observation. We read the biblical text thoughtfully. We read in order to understand, and that requires us to pay attention to the details while also looking for the big picture. Bible study is a process of discovery, and discovery is always a powerful experience.

Experts have broken the process of Bible study into three stages: 1) observation; 2) interpretation; and 3) application. We read the biblical text asking, "What is it saying?"(observation) "What does it mean?" (interpretation), and "How does it make an impact today?"(application). This is as important as anything else we will cover in this book. This is a method of Bible study, but it also a way of reading the Bible with our brains fully functioning—a mindset that will lead us into the depths of the gold mine.

There's a temptation to skip to the third question, application, in order to get the big payoff. But it is only the true meaning of Scripture that impacts our lives, not a random association with its words. We have to do the work of observation first. It's not too difficult. Every Bible reader can sharpen his or her observational skills.

So what are we looking for as we observe the text?

1. *The basic questions: who, what, when, where, why, how.* These are the same questions a good journalist, physician, attorney, or detective will ask when approaching a new situation. When we know it is the apostle Paul (who) instructing people on worship (what) in his later years (when) writing about the needs of the Ephesian church (where) because of false teaching (why) via a courier (how), we understand the

context of all the strong statements Paul makes about worship in 1 Timothy. Every answer to those six questions is different when we look at the heart-rending confession in Psalm 51, or the oracles of Jeremiah, or the visions of Revelation.

2. *Emphasis and repetition.* Any section of the biblical text has main points and minor points. When a biblical author tells us what the main point of a passage is, sometimes by repeating the basic idea again and again, our powers of observation should focus on that point.

3. *Key words and phrases.* When we read a passage there are typically a few key words or phrases upon which the whole passage hangs. What is grammatically dominant may help, but sometimes the key expression is buried in the middle of the text, or comes at the end.

4. *Comparisons and contrasts.* Biblical passages frequently compare one truth to another, or draw a contrast between a truth and a falsehood. When we read Jesus' parable of the soils, we compare and contrast the experience of people who are like the hard soil, the thorny soil, the shallow soil, or the good soil. The truth of the passage is contained in the contrasts. Jesus frequently made comparisons, too. The kingdom of God is like a mustard seed, or leaven, or treasure hidden in a field. Jesus said of himself: "I am the good shepherd," "I am the bread sent from heaven," "I am the light of the world."

5. *Cause and effect.* Many biblical passages describe what happens when someone makes a terrible error, or makes a truly good decision or commitment. Such connections are not always absolute. What is said in Proverbs, for instance, is generally true. The oft-quoted Proverbs 22:6, "Start children off on the way they should go, and even when they are old they will not turn from it," is true most of the time, but not absolutely. A proverb is different from a promise.

There are many other details in a given passage that the good Bible detective will observe and note. If we read Scripture in this way we are more likely to see the deep meaning of it, and we will avoid getting thrown off track by a superficial reading.

Poor observation can be the result of laziness, or a habit of taking the words of Scripture passages and using them as springboards to go wherever our whim carries us (this applies to plenty of Bible teachers and preachers as well). Good observation is zeal to understand the text with respect for the intent of the author to communicate something specific and helpful.

Chapter 6

CURIOSITY

They spent months digging in the inhospitable sands of Egypt, searching for clues and watching for concealed chambers. One day, down a 30-foot passageway, Howard Carter and a few workmen discovered a door, and when they cut a small hole, Carter peered in and saw "wonderful things." It turned out to be the famous tomb of King Tut. Breaking into the chamber, they discovered elaborate vases, couches, statues, jewelry, chariots, a beautiful ostrich feather fan that stood in perfect condition, and, of course, the solid gold coffin of Tutankhamen.

Howard Carter grew up in England in the late 1800's, a weak and sickly boy who possessed a powerful sense of curiosity. That curiosity is what drove him years later to the sands of Egypt.

Treasure is discovered not by casual people, but by explorers who are driven by the belief that there is untouched richness, and that it is worth the work to find it. So it is with Bible study. The people who find the treasures of God's word are those who are driven by faith and curiosity, and are committed to doing the work.

Browsing casually through the Bible will not yield its deepest treasure. Bible study is the study of God, and we are not longing to know God if we are only giving casual glances his way.

Neither does this work: always and only going to the Bible to find solutions to our problems. It does not work in marriage when husband or wife sees the other only as a solution to life's problems. Marriage is to be an ever-deepening knowledge of each other. And so God invites us to listen to his word, to explore its depths and find its treasures, not just as an answer book, but as a deep and personal conversation.

Really good journalists are driven by curiosity about their subjects, not about how they will be viewed by the public. Scientists have integrity when they examine the evidence, no matter where it takes them. The person you call your best friend is probably someone who is genuinely interested in you, not just someone who wants to take advantage of you.

Some people are naturally curious. They connect with others easily because they are interested, which shows respect. They read about a wide range of subjects. They open the Bible like an archaeologist digging in the sand.

But most people have to choose to be curious. In Bible study it is about faith, the choice to believe that there is a treasure of truth in Scripture, and the desire to dig it out. It is about respecting God, and thus respecting his word. Jesus said the person whose heart is like the soil on the path—the shallow soil—will never see the fruit of God's truth. The work of God begins with our openness to receiving scripture deeply into our minds and hearts.

Here are some practical steps to make sure we are approaching the Bible with the commitment of curiosity:

1. *Do not rush reading and studying Scripture.* Better to spend more time on smaller passages than to hurry through chapters looking only for the big, obvious points. There is a time for reading through the Bible quickly (I love the 90-day Bible reading plans), but that must be paired with slow reading and careful study.

2. *Pretend you have never read it before.* Bible comprehension is cumulative over a lifetime, but it is good to apply a fresh eye every time we look at a passage, otherwise our eye will only be attracted to what we've seen and underlined before.

3. *Understand your level of expertise.* If you're not an archaeologist, you are not in a place to evaluate the

findings of archaeological surveys in the Middle East. If you are not a botanist or a geologist or a medical researcher, you are dependent on the knowledge we get from those who are. If you have not spent years studying Hebrew or Greek, you cannot reach conclusions on your own about matters of lexicography or grammar. This is why reference works like Bible dictionaries, encyclopedias, and commentaries are crucial in Bible study. But we must avoid the temptation to only consult those experts whose conclusions we prefer for one reason or another. We must look for good authority on these matters. (Much more about this later.)

4. *Have confidence in your curiosity.* Know that it is better to ask a lot of questions, even if they seem unintelligent, than to be incurious. Trust that your respectful and curiosity-driven study of Scripture is at the heart of good Bible comprehension. Yes, we need experts on detailed matters of history and language and culture. But good old-fashioned study and inductive thought, driven by natural inquisitiveness, will reveal to us the essential meaning of the biblical text, and anyone can do that.

We are all able to peek inside and see "wonderful things."

Chapter 7

UNDERSTANDING THE INTENT
OF THE BIBLICAL AUTHORS

Everybody wants to be respected. A mature person does not expect everyone to agree with him or her, or have the same temperament, or even the same beliefs, but we want other people to respect us, to see who we are, to understand our values and our motivations. This type of respect comes only through listening and knowing.

Any serious approach to Bible study must be founded on respect for the Bible and respect for the intent of its authors. Any of us may pick up the Bible and let the words bounce on the kindling of our minds like sparks, hoping a nice little fire will start. This is the easy way, treating the words of Scripture almost like magic or like a secret code. But what Scripture offers is far more profound and life-changing. It is truth, massive and multi-faceted, about all of life, communicated through the actual lives of its authors in their real-life settings.

The truth of God's word has been passed on to us through the stories and the teachings of his chosen spokespeople. Whether we are looking at historical narratives, wisdom teaching, prophecy, gospels, or epistles, the words were written down by people inspired by the Holy Spirit of God. These people were not merely keyboards. The prophets and apostles did not sit around waiting for divine words to pop into their heads. They spoke with genuine and specific intent, which was to deliver the truth of God to their audiences—directly, clearly, deeply—and our study of Scripture all these centuries later must include a reverence for the Bible as the word of the living God which has been transmitted through the words (and the lives, experiences, and commitments) of the biblical authors.

It works like this: you're studying 1 Corinthians, and you observe in the opening words who wrote it, to whom he wrote it, and the occasion for him writing it. As you study along you come upon many issues—marriage, divorce, morality, church leadership, spiritual gifts, social relationships—and you continually ask yourself, "What did the Apostle Paul mean by this?" "Why did he raise that issue?" "What are the believers in Corinth asking him?" "What did he want to happen among them?" "Why did he use the specific words he chose?"

Some of the answers come easily, right out of the text. Others require deeper study. Either way, our posture as Bible students must be, "What did this author mean in writing these particular words to that particular audience at that particular time?" We do not ask, "What does this mean to me?" Because, as has often been pointed out, the Bible can never mean what it never meant. In other words, we have to focus on the original meaning first, and that has to do with the intent of the author.

In 1 Corinthians, the Apostle Paul intended to correct serious problems in a Christian community situated in an immoral culture. In Jeremiah, the prophet was warning God's people to return to faith and recommit to God. Acts is the intentional work of a man named Luke who wanted to lay down an accurate report of what had happened after the ministry of Jesus, an extension of his "orderly account" of the life of Jesus in the Gospel we call Luke. The Psalms are patterns for worship and prayer. Proverbs is a set of guidelines for living a wise life and avoiding foolishness in all its forms.

And so it goes, biblical book by biblical book. Dozens of authors. Locations spread around the whole Mediterranean world and the empires of Mesopotamia.

Audiences that included true believers, lapsed followers, and people disconnected from God.

Our lives in the 21st century may be far removed from the world the biblical authors occupied. But the core issues of human existence and meaning do not change. Our vices and virtues, foolishness and wisdom, corruptions and characters have not changed over the millennia.

It is a privilege to study this word. It does take work and awareness. It takes a careful, listening ear. That is where respect happens. And when we respect what someone has tried to tell us, we can comprehend its true meaning.

When we find out "what it meant" at the time it was written, then we can move on to "what it means" in terms of timeless principles. And then, and only then, can we ask, "How does it apply to our lives today?" If we approach the text with respect for God and with respect for the authors of Scripture, we will find substance and power which a superficial reading could never yield.

Part II

THE WAYS OF STUDYING THE BIBLE

Chapter 8

THE MANY GENRES
OF SCRIPTURE

There is a large bookstore I frequently visit. I know just where to find histories and biographies, novels and picture books, technical manuals and reference works. I would be lost in the bookstore unless I understood the different genres in its various sections, so I can zoom in on what I am looking for.

And when I open the Bible, I know from having studied it for a long time whether I am reading a gospel passage, a prophecy, a Psalm, or an epistle. I do not expect Isaiah to describe the history of Israel—for that I'd turn to the books of Kings and Chronicles. When I'm studying a Psalm, I know that the forms of a poem or song will help me understand the meaning.

And when I read 1 Corinthians, I know I'm listening to one side of a two-sided conversation.

One of the most powerful and complex features of the Bible is that it consists of many different types, or genres, of texts.

The major genres of Scripture include the following:

1. *Narrative*

This includes books of the Bible or sections of books which simply tell the story of what happened. Exodus is an expansive, epic narrative. Ruth focusses on the story of one family. Acts recounts the spectacular events of the first generation of Christians as they were led and inspired by the Holy Spirit. Narratives tell us what happened, according to the purposes of the author. Sometimes there are spiritual lessons to be gleaned from these events. Other times we are just gaining the context of the history of God's people.

2. *Poetry*

This is all of Psalms and sections of other books. The power of poetry comes through the use of vivid figurative language ("As the deer pants for streams of water, so my soul pants for you, my God" Ps. 42:1). Also, ideas are repeated, sometimes with the same words, other times with synonyms (synonymous parallelism). The Psalms and other poetic sections of the Bible do communicate ideas, but most of all they express emotion. They show life in its fullness.

3. *Wisdom*

Proverbs, Job, and Ecclesiastes are collections of wise sayings meant to shape the moral and ethical lives of their readers. They cover many practical topics including communication, friendship, marriage, money, temptation, aging, illness, death, faith, and much more. The book of James in the New Testament functions in many ways like Proverbs in the Old Testament.

4. *Prophecy*

The books of the four major prophets (Isaiah, Jeremiah, Ezekiel, Daniel) and the 12 minor prophets (Hosea through Malachi) are all God's word to his covenant people, warning them and bolstering them during periods of pronounced spiritual and national danger. They are mostly oracles (verbal pronouncements), later written down. In the prophetic books, we gain spiritual lessons about the disposition of God (disappointed, indignant, sorrowful, tender, caring), and the condition of the people addressed (frightened, disobedient, humbled, arrogant). We must first read Old Testament prophetic books as God's challenge to the original audiences, and then we can apply the lessons to our day.

5. *Gospels*

Matthew, Mark, Luke, and John are similar to the genres of narrative or biography, but they go beyond telling the story of what happened. The Gospels are proclamation. The people who wrote them were true believers relating first-hand accounts of the life and teachings of Jesus. And so we read the genre of Gospel as faith documents, announcing a world-changing event centered in the person of Jesus. Gospels include narrative, but also other specialized literary forms like parables, which are lessons embedded in extended similes and metaphors.

6. *Epistles*

The letters of the New Testament were communications to specific individuals or groups either to solve problems or encourage. The apostle Paul meant Romans to be an overarching description of Christian faith, whereas 1 Corinthians was occasioned by problems, including a list of questions the believers in Corinth had for Paul ("Now concerning the matters you wrote about," 1 Cor. 7:1), and the letters to Timothy were intended to encourage and guide a young church leader in a challenging spot. Epistles are "occasioned" texts, and so we need to understand the circumstances that motivated the author to write.

7. *Apocalypse*

The book of Revelation and parts of the book of Daniel are revelations. Like other prophecies, they proclaim urgent messages to their original audiences—in particular, warning and comfort. They employ symbolic language to a greater degree than other prophetic books. To understand these symbols, we can study similar expressions used elsewhere in Scripture.

When we sit down to study the Bible, we must first recognize what genre we are looking at. If we don't account for the type of biblical book we're reading, we will certainly misunderstand and misapply the truth of God's word. These different but complementary genres also demonstrate that God's word is wide and varied and deep, and worthy of a lifetime of study.

For more on the genres of Scripture, see chapters 6 through 23 of *How to Understand the Bible* (WordWay, 2015).

Chapter 9

APPROACHING A BIBLICAL BOOK

The reason we study the Bible is to deepen our connection with our Creator, who has graciously spoken to us through the prophets and apostles. The way we establish that connection is by looking for the true meaning of the biblical text, which we can only get to if we examine the whole before the parts.

The basic block of meaning in the Bible is the individual book. These books have different forms: a chronicle of history (for example, Joshua), a collection of prophetic oracles (e.g., Isaiah), a collection of worship poems and songs (e.g., Psalms), a gospel proclamation (e.g., Luke), a personal letter (e.g., Titus), the account of a vision of great earthly drama (e.g., Revelation), etc.

When we prepare to study a book of the Bible, whether for personal Bible study, group participation, or teaching, we need to understand the following:

1. *The historical background of the book.* For instance: the first five books of the Bible were written in order to give the people of God a clear vision of who they were; Ezra and Nehemiah were written to remind people of important core spiritual values as they began to rebuild a nation; Lamentations comes out of the utter loss and humiliation of conquest; the apostle Paul wrote Philippians while he was a prisoner of the Roman Empire; Revelation came out at a time of great persecution. Each of these historical settings helps us understand the meaning of the texts.

2. *The cultural background of the book.* The culture of a people is made up of their beliefs, customs, languages, arts, and ways of life. Culture is deep and complex. Biblical authors were writing while living in particular cultures, and we must understand those cultures in order to recognize how they influence the biblical text. The Hebrews moved into and conquered the people of Canaan, and the clash between their cultures was at the center of the biblical story for centuries. We need to understand the paganism and idolatry and tribalism of the times. To understand the Gospel of Matthew, we have to account for some details about Jewish, Greek, and Roman culture. 1 Corinthians requires us to know something about the social immorality of Greek cul-

ture, while the book of Hebrews brings up cultural aspects of first century Judaism.

3. *The geographical setting of the book.* Most of the prophets in the Old Testament spoke to God's people in Israel and Judah, but the writings of Ezekiel in exile in Babylonia have an entirely different geographical setting which needs to be taken into account when we try to understand the words. Books written from a rural setting use rural metaphors, and those written from urban settings use urban language and comparisons. Geography matters.

4. *The political setting of the book.* Writings coming out of a strong empire like Israel during the days of David and Solomon have one set of concerns. Those written during horrible civil war have a different perspective. And those written from exile take the perspective of the conquered and oppressed.

The books of the Bible were written by different people living in different cultural environments, but these varying backgrounds do not make the Bible impossible to understand, nor do they obscure the core meaning of Scripture. In fact, the multifaceted historical, cultural, geographical, and political backgrounds of biblical books make them richer as records of God's truth. We learn about moral value and spiritual principles as God reveals them in all of life's circumstances. Also, when we acknowledge all the complexities of the backgrounds of the biblical books, we are learning all the ways God Almighty is redeeming and judging the human race.

What are the steps to approaching biblical books as whole units? Here is one process:

1. *Begin by reading a simple introduction to the biblical book you are about to study.* Such introductions are found in study Bibles or Bible handbooks.

2. *Read the whole book straight through, ignoring chapter and verse divisions.* Those divisions were added many centuries later, and they can get in the way of a simple, straight reading.

3. *Take notes.* The questions you have, the statements that stun you, the words that are repeated, the transitions that show the flow and connection within the book. Watch for the main points. Perceive the passions and concerns of the writer.

4. *Make an outline.* Don't worry about the outlines produced by Bible scholars at this point. This is your personal perception of the flow and structure of the biblical book. Your outline can simply be a list of the main parts and points in the book.

5. *Read a more detailed background resource.* This could be a book introduction in a commentary, an online article, or an article in a Bible encyclopedia.

6. *Go back and read the whole book again.* If you're teaching it, read the book a third time (and a fourth time, and a fifth time). Your listeners will benefit from your intimacy with the text. It is amazing how much

more we pick up as we scan through the biblical text repeatedly.

Spending time examining a biblical book as a whole gets us past fragmented reading. "A verse a day" will never get us to the meaning of the Bible. We need to keep seeing the whole.

Chapter 10

UNDERSTANDING THE FLOW OF MEANING OF A BIBLICAL BOOK

Before I travel to a new city I study a map of the whole area. I note the natural boundaries—ocean, desert, open land, or other cities—then I observe the major highways that traverse or loop the city. I concentrate on the places I'm going to visit, and let that image get imprinted on my mind.

I know this sounds old-fashioned in a day when GPS can give us turn-by-turn directions, but I've learned the hard way that if I don't have any general idea of where I'm going, I might drive to an entirely mistaken location.

In order to sense the substance of an entire biblical book before we get to verse-by-verse study, we need to accurately perceive the flow of meaning of the biblical book we are studying. I say "flow" because most biblical books progress from one idea to the next along a trajectory of real meaning. A book may tell a story (narrative), or offer oracles (prophecy), or develop teaching (epistles). To grasp the meaning, we need to understand the logical flow of the author. Like driving a car, we go from one road to the next; there is a journey—a flow—as we travel between locations. We understand where we are by knowing where we have been, and by anticipating the next set of turns ahead of us. (There are some biblical books that do not have a chapter-by-chapter logical progression, like the book of Psalms, which is a collection of songs and poems.)

What we do at this level of Bible study is outline. This can be one of the most fruitful personal exercises. Forget the outline you find in your study Bible or commentary or dictionary; just read the book through for yourself. Then read it again, noting the large logical sections. This is like studying the map for yourself, rather than relying on the GPS to give you turn-by-turn directions. This is how most biblical authors intended for their audiences to engage with the text. The epistles that were addressed to churches, for instance, were in many cases read out loud in the congregations—from beginning to end, in all probability. The original audiences heard the whole, and could comprehend the major points of meaning.

After you come up with your own outline, you can compare that with the outlines of scholars.

Let's use Genesis as an example. Reading the book all the way through in one day, even if not in one sitting, gives us a perspective of the whole map. Because it's mostly narrative, we can see its stories broken down into 1) the early stories of the world (primeval history) from Creation through the Flood; 2) the story of Abraham; 3) the story of Jacob; and 4) the story of Joseph. As we read, we look for markers of meaning, which may be statements that describe the whole or connect the parts. What God says to Abraham about making his descendants into a great nation, and that through him all the nations of the earth would be blessed, is a bird's-eye view of the whole. Often, a book's beginning and ending will provide clues for overall meaning. The Creation account is not just about the world being created—it's about a people. Genesis 50 concludes with Abraham's descendants beginning to multiply, although they're displaced in the land of Egypt—another great theme of the Bible: God's people in a foreign place.

The epistle of 1 Corinthians in the New Testament has its own unique flow of meaning. After Paul gives the customary greeting, affirming the divine calling of the church and asserting his own apostolic authority, he confronts the Corinthian church about their scandalous divisions (chapters 1-4). Then he asserts the moral standards Christians ought to follow (chapters 5-6), after which we see an important connecting statement: "Now for the matters you wrote about" (7:1). This is the structural clue that helps us follow Paul's transition from one topic (marriage, worship, discipleship) to the next (replying to the church leaders' questions).

Here is what we need to be looking for as we seek to understand the flow of meaning in a biblical book:

1. *Repetition* - Themes mentioned frequently may reveal the intent of the author.

2. *Connections* - Biblical books frequently have obvious connecting statements that reveal the logic of the flow.

3. *Major statements* - Statements that summarize overall meaning are like landmarks along the highway, but we may not notice them until we've read the book several times.

4. *Parallels* - Ideas that are repeated in cycles may signal that the meaning is to be found in the patterns (like the sets of seven in the book of Revelation, for instance).

If you're creating an outline of the book you're approaching, it can be in the traditional form of major points, subpoints, sub-sub points, etc., but this is not the only way to record the flow of meaning, especially if the book has no such structure. To document the flow, it may be best to list the major points and the subsidiary points in whatever form feels intuitive to you. Our main purpose is to document the overall logic of a text, listing the major points, the transitional steps, and the important sets of meaning in order to comprehend the author's flow of thinking. The most important part of this exercise is to simply write down the book's major ideas.

As much as we can, we should ignore the chapter and verse designations in our Bibles. These markers were added centuries after the biblical texts were written. They may signal an accurate division of meaning and flow, but oftentimes they do not.

What about the section headings that the Bible translators and editors include in the final form of Bibles published today? If you're using a good quality modern translation, those headings can be helpful. They represent the Bible editor's best attempt at breaking down the major blocks of meaning. But if you want to do your own fresh reading of the biblical text, read a Bible that excludes chapter and verse numbers and section headings.

It is deeply satisfying to read and re-read and study a particular book and to gain a real familiarity with the locations of meaning in the text. It's like getting to know a new city, not just by memorizing a map, but by using the map to actually travel the streets and highways. Note the landmarks and boundaries, and you'll know where you are the next time you visit.

Chapter 11

STUDYING A PARTICULAR BIBLE PASSAGE

In the last two chapters, we looked at approaching a whole book of the Bible, which we do in order to understand overall context. After that we considered the importance of understanding the flow of meaning of a biblical book through some form of outlining. Now we look at studying particular passages.

As a practical matter, our study of the Bible typically comes down to peering intently into a specific passage. So, bearing in mind the importance of the whole-book context and meaning, how then do we plunge into a passage to understand and apply?

What we typically mean by a "passage" is a segment of a biblical book that holds together in some meaningful way. That may be just two or three verses, or a chapter or two. The chapter and verse numbers in the Bible we are all familiar with were not developed for the biblical text until the 13th through the 16th centuries. They are helpful, but we should not consider them definitive divisions of meaning.

Paragraph divisions are typical for most Bible editions, which are an attempt to show blocks of thought. Most Bible editions also include section headings, created by the translators to flag blocks of meaning. These are helpful, but we should remember that they were not in the original text of the Bible.

The practicality of looking at one biblical passage at a time is sometimes a function of teaching or preaching. A pastor can offer a sermon that summarizes the whole book of Jeremiah, for instance, but it's much more helpful to select a chapter, or a segment of meaning that's just a few verses long. A sermon or a teaching could be based on Jeremiah 31, but it may be better to focus on Jeremiah 31, verses 31-35, the passage that describes "the new covenant." These five verses are like the Rosetta Stone, a key that unlocks the meaning of the old and the new covenant. There are many details in those few verses, each of enormous importance, and each requiring study to get the meaning of the words and phrases. "I will make a new covenant." "I will put my law in their minds and write it on their hearts." "No longer will they teach their neighbor... because they will all know me." "I will forgive their wickedness and will remember their sins no more."

Let's say you have identified a passage to focus on. Perhaps the Bible study group you attend has planned to focus on Hebrews 11, and you want to put in some personal study before the group meets.

In the case of Hebrews 11, the chapter designation is quite helpful. It begins with the magnificent statement: "Now faith is confidence in what we hope for and assurance about what we do not see." You read the chapter once, slowly and naturally, and then you go back and read it again. And a third time. The first time you just read. By the third time you are underlining or highlighting (if that is how you best learn), or you make brief notes. You may choose to read it aloud. It is amazing how much we see in a passage that way. (People in the ancient world typically did not read silently.)

As you read and reread, the text of this discreet passage is getting stuck in your head. It is a long enough passage to have context, but short enough that you can go over it again and again. You notice some important ideas only on your third or fourth reading. Diligence is a friend of observation.

Through simple reading you observe the structure of the passage. The introductory truth about faith in verse 1, followed by a string of notable Old Testament figures who demonstrated deep faith. You see that there is an intense conclusion (verses 32-38) to this roll call of heroes of faith, a vivid description of the cost of faith in torture and martyrdom. And then, in verse 39, a broad truth: these people were commended for their faith, "yet none of them received what had been promised." This is faith. Believing, not just possessing. Now that is a truth—a major truth—that can be applied in powerful ways in our lives (we'll get to application later).

That is, in fact, the next step in Hebrews. Chapter 12 gives a profound real-life application. "Let us throw off everything that hinders and the sin that so easily entangles. And let us run with perseverance the race marked out for us, fixing our eyes on Jesus, the pioneer and perfecter of faith" (12:1-2).

Studying or teaching a passage like Hebrews 11 is incredibly powerful when we take the time to consider the details.

This is why focusing on just one verse of Scripture at a time is inadequate and even dangerous. The meaning of single sentences can only come out of the wider context in which they are found. It is not wrong to feature a single verse as the highlight of a passage, a portion that is easy to memorize, as long as we remember that the biblical authors themselves intended us to understand the whole of what they were saying.

We need to focus on complete thoughts when we study Scripture, so taking one passage at a time ensures we will derive the intended meaning of the author.

Chapter 12

THE MEANING OF SPECIFIC
WORDS IN THE BIBLE

It is amazing, when you think about it, that you can write a single word on a piece of paper, show it to someone else, and produce in that person's mind the idea of the object, action, or concept that single word represents. Whether you write *lion, moon, wedding, run, or war*—in an instant, a single written word connects your mind with the mind of another person. This is the incredible power of words.

But specific words often have multiple possible meanings. What if you write the word *bar*? The other person may imagine a long metal rod, or a piece of candy, or a room in a hotel where alcohol is served, or a court of law, or a musical notation. All are meanings of the word *bar*. And what if the other person comes from another country where the meaning of a word is entirely different, or even offensive?

Studying the Bible inevitably involves studying the meaning of individual words, but we must always remember that the intent of the biblical authors is found in complete thoughts—we find the meaning of words in their context. The word *white* can mean a color, or quality, or race; the word *house* can mean a home or a business establishment or a dynasty. But put them together—white house—and you have a specific idea. Or change it to White House and you know you're talking about one particular building in Washington, D.C.

Let's say you're studying John, chapter 1, a passage packed with amazing truths. We find words which we need to understand: beginning, Word, life, light, children of God, born of God, flesh, dwelling, grace, truth, Son. We may assume that some of these words have obvious meanings, but still we will benefit from learning all we can about them.

Most words have a range of possible meanings, what linguists call a "semantic range." The word *flesh*, for instance, in a biblical passage may refer to the physical body, or it can mean humanity (as in "flesh and blood"), or the word "flesh" may refer to limited human nature, or it can refer to the sinfulness of human nature. The same is true of *word* in John 1. The Greek term *logos* can mean expression, or rationality, or a single word. *Logos* was also used at the time by certain philosophical schools for the idea of a universal power that holds the universe together. By calling Jesus "the Word," John may have been saying that in Jesus we find the fulfillment and personification of "the word of the Lord" in the Old Testament, or that Jesus is a better alternative to the cosmic Logos of the philosophers, or both. So much is at stake in the meaning of a word—even the word *word*!

So how do we study the meaning of the words of Scripture? Here is where we rely on the expertise of linguists whose job it is to take the Hebrew, Aramaic, and Greek words of the Bible and compare their use within the Bible and with outside sources. Linguists produce lexicons or dictionaries—tools that summarize the findings of these extensive comparisons. As we have said before, one of the most useful Bible study tools is a good Bible dictionary or encyclopedia. These tools will summarize the meaning of names, geography, theology, and every other kind of word. From Caesarea to coin, remnant to resurrection, Baal to Bethel, heaven to heart, Judas to justification. Bible dictionaries are immensely valuable (see the list of Bible dictionaries and encyclopedias at www.WordWay.org/HowToStudyTheBible).

When you look up a word in such a tool, use it as an opportunity to learn about that word's whole range of meaning throughout the Bible. This you can file away in the back of your mind for future reference. But do not make the mistake of believing that any one use of a word in any one passage includes that word's full semantic range of meaning. When someone uses the word *bar* you do not think he or she is using every possible meaning of the word. Context tells you specifically what the person means. So it is in Bible study. The word *world* can mean the earth, or humanity, or the sinfulness of humanity. You can tell from the context. The word *judge* may be God's act of justice, or God as judge, or one of the leaders in the book of Judges, or the act of harshly criticizing others. You can tell from the context.

And then there is the issue of synonyms. The English word *love* in the New Testament is often used in translations for three of the four Greek words for love: *agape, philia,* and *eros.*

The other tool that helps us determine what a specific word means in a specific context is the commentary. A Bible commentary is an explanation of the biblical text by someone (usually a scholar) who has immersed himself or herself in the language, context, and form of biblical texts. The Bible commentator reveals details that we simply don't see in our simple reading of Scripture, like archaeological discoveries, historical details, linguistic particularities, and details about geography and culture.

The commentator has looked at the full semantic range of all of the words in a passage, and will indicate which specific meanings are intended by the author, excluding other possibilities. And if the deeper meaning of a word is important, a good commentator will unpack that. (More about commentaries later.)

We should not be surprised that getting at the meaning of the words of Scripture involves some work, though the basic meaning of a biblical text is typically obvious with simple reading. We have to work at times in the same way that we work at any relationship worth having. Words are gifts, and they lead ultimately to God himself.

Chapter 13

DO WE NEED TO KNOW HEBREW AND GREEK?

After listening to teachers and preachers who refer to the "original" Hebrew and Greek texts of Scripture, telling us about hidden messages, we may have gotten the impression that the true meaning of Scripture is veiled to those who can't read ancient languages.

This is tragic. Believers need to plunge into the study of the Bible, confident that the word of the eternal God—and its specific meanings—is available to us. Otherwise we will have divided the Christian community into the elites who know the languages of God and the masses who are dependent on those elites.

Some of us did learn Hebrew and Greek in our training to become pastors, and we use that knowledge judiciously as we study biblical texts. But a wise person told me a long time ago that it is not fair to a congregation if we continually allude to the meaning of the "original" biblical texts, because all that does is tell people that the Bible is a huge step removed from them, which is not true.

This is important. If you use a Bible translation that came from the diligent work of Bible scholars who know how to do the work of linguistics and textual analysis and translation, you are indeed holding the word of God in your hand. The vast, sweeping story of God and the human race in Scripture reveals the truth of God in the big, bold, repeated propositions. The fine points are important, but minor points must always be interpreted in the light of major points. And the major meaning of Scripture, including specific passages, is rendered well in careful, responsible translations.

What about all the allusions to Hebrew and Greek and Aramaic meanings in the Bible study tools we use? What are we to make of the commentaries, Bible dictionaries, and other tools that speak about the meanings we get from the original languages? And what do we do when different tools make differing points about the original languages?

If you do not know Hebrew or Greek, it is not your responsibility to make decisions about translation issues. We let the experts do that. The best thing you can do is use a reputable commentary or Bible dictionary or handbook in the first place. Take the benefit of what those Bible scholars have presented, but always place the finer points in subservience to the major points.

Note that some commentaries go from one Hebrew or Greek phrase to the next. These "technical" commentaries may be awkward to use if one does not know Hebrew or Greek. Many commentaries only allude to the original languages where it is important.

You may have noticed footnotes in your Bible that say something like, "Some manuscripts say..." Such notes mean that the Bible translators have had access to many different ancient manuscripts and there is a judgment call about which variation is likely to have been what the original author wrote. (We do not have the original manuscripts of any biblical book, so we rely on copies. More accurately, copies of copies of copies.)

Those notes come from Bible scholars who believe it is important to mention that there is an alternative wording in the Hebrew or Greek of a passage. These instances are few and far between, and never does a major doctrine of the faith hang on which Hebrew or Greek wording was most likely original. We have some textual variants because scholars are working with the thousands of Hebrew and Greek manuscripts that we have from the ancient world. They compare them with great precision in order to determine what the original text would have been (since no one possesses the papyrus Matthew or Paul or James wrote on).

Here is the big picture. The Bible is the word of God, delivered up in the form of thousands and thousands of words combined into strings that confer meaning. For thousands of years, the Bible has been a revelation of God that has transformed lives and shaped history. The main meanings of the word of God have held people together with their specific revelations, even though there are doctrinal differences between believers.

The Bible itself says that God was intent to speak to us through the prophets and the apostles, and through his Son, the Lord Jesus, and with the inspiration and illumination of the Holy Spirit (Hebrews 1:1-4). The books of the Bible may have been written in Hebrew and Greek and Aramaic, but their meaning is available to us all, and we benefit from the diligent work of Bible scholars who guide us on the fine points.

[Bible translations and Bible study tools are discussed in greater detail in *How to Understand the Bible*, WordWay, 2015.]

Chapter 14

DEVELOPING OUR BIBLICAL VOCABULARY

In the previous chapter we looked at the importance of the meaning of specific words in the Bible. Individual words are building blocks, but we do not discover the rich meaning and truth of God's word just by looking at individual words. We find the meaning in the statements and ideas that the biblical authors gave us in complete expressions (sentences or groups of sentences). And even those ideas can be grasped only by viewing them in the wider context of the biblical book they are embedded in.

Nevertheless, we have to be able to study words in order to get at the whole meaning. Or at least we need to understand how the translators decided which words in the receptor language (English, for instance) best represent the original meaning (in Hebrew or Greek).

None of us need to pretend we are linguists and lexicographers. That work has been done for us by people who have worked hard for many years in those disciplines. I learned Greek and Hebrew in graduate school, but that does not make me a linguist or lexicographer, which are highly skilled disciplines.

Here is the point: the ordinary Bible student does not need to judge the subtleties of translation alternatives when studying the words of a specific biblical passage. Yes, we can note the various translations, or even the details of the semantic range of a given word, but unless you have spent many years immersed in studying Hebrew or Greek, it is not your responsibility to judge the translation options.

It is important for us to have confidence in our Bible translations. We all will decide what version we prefer to use. Some prefer word-for-word (sometimes referred to as "literal") translations. These translations let the reader know the specific word choice and phraseology of the biblical author, but sometimes are more difficult to read because they may not have the flow of the way we use language today. Other people gravitate toward what may be called thought-for-thought translations. And then there are paraphrases or free translations which take whole sentences and render them in the colloquial use of language.

[For more about specific Bible translations, go to www.WordWay.org/HowToStudyTheBible]

If you are studying a passage and there are some words that are pivotal for the meaning of the text, how do you drill down on the meaning of those words? By using the tools that expert linguists and lexicographers have put in our hands:

1. *Look at how three or four different Bible translations have rendered the word* (you can look at many translations in an online resource like BibleGateway.com, or computer Bible programs). Perhaps the same English word or phrase is used uniformly. If not, you will learn something by noting how different translators rendered it.

2. *Use a concordance* (or an online tool like Bible-Gateway.com, where you can use "keyword search") to glance through a list of verses using the word you are curious about. Just remember that the word in English may be the translation of several different Hebrew or Greek words. (There are concordance functions that allow you to focus on only one specific Hebrew or Greek word.)

2. *Look up the word in a Bible dictionary or encyclopedia.* If "baptize" is in your passage, you'll learn the linguistic meaning of the word, its historical usage, and its use in a wide range of biblical books. There are not many uses of the word in the New Testament, so you can go and look them up yourself as well. Just make

sure you don't assume that the word's entire semantic range of meaning is included in any one passage. Note that some dictionaries specialize in theological words (see resources at www.WordWay.org/HowToStudy-TheBible).

3. *If the word is really pivotal, a detailed commentary will explain the meaning of the word* (more about commentaries later). The commentator is leaning on the research of linguists and lexicographers and giving us summary meanings. You are not likely to find word studies in one-volume commentaries, but you will in commentaries devoted to single biblical books.

As life-long students of the Bible, we are continually growing our biblical vocabulary. Our understanding of the words of Scripture grows both wider (as we link many passages) and deeper (as we take time to study the words with the tools available to us). We gain a language of revelation, with the light of truth becoming brighter and brighter. We do not do this in order to be arrogant or elitist. We study in order to know God, and to better explain the ways and the will of God to others. Jesus warned some experts in Scripture that they knew the words but had missed the meaning (Matthew 22:29). That is what we want to avoid.

Chapter 15

TWO APPROACHES: DISCOVERY
AND QUESTIONS

There are two basic ways we get to know the word of God. The first way is to come to Scripture with an attitude of discovery, letting the words of the biblical authors have their impact. In this approach, we allow the word of God to set the agenda, form the issues, shape the questions, determine the emphases. This is when we read Exodus and see new things about God's love and power, or we read a Psalm and get a fresh sense of the main heart issues that come through, or we read 2 Corinthians and understand the angst out of which Paul approaches a church that has given him many headaches. Reading the Bible in this way is true discovery. It is a spiritual attitude that says: *God, my mind*

and heart are open. Say what you will, tear down what you will, build what you will.

The other way we study the word of God is to come to it with our questions. Your friend wants to divorce her husband, and you go to Scripture to see what it says about grounds for divorce. Your church gives you the option of having your newborn baptized or waiting until he or she can express faith, and you wonder: what does Scripture actually say about baptism? Your country is about to go to war, and you think there must be a difference between just war and unjust war —but what does Scripture say about it?

Both approaches are valid, and both build us up in different ways. If we only use the first method, we will miss opportunities to go searching for principles on which to make good decisions. But if we only come to Scripture with our questions (the second approach) we will never let God have the first word, and we will miss the big ideas of Scripture that our questions would never anticipate.

The best long-term way to build a superstructure of faith is to strengthen our belief system through the first, open-to-discovery approach to the Bible. But yet there are times when it's appropriate and wise to go to Scripture with our questions, looking for answers. So how do we approach Scripture with our questions?

There are proper methods and deeply flawed methods. For instance, it is a mistake to go to the Bible hunting for a single verse that perhaps God will use to solve a dilemma we're in. If you're deciding whether to take that job in Cincinnati and you happen upon a passage where God tells someone to "go forth," that is not a biblical answer to your question.

We can find good answers in Scripture when we ask questions of principle. For instance:

What is the meaning of sin?

What principles should govern my personal finances?

What is the basis of a good marriage?

What should I be trying to do in worship?

Am I responsible for the mistakes of my kids?

What is the work of the Holy Spirit?

What does it mean to be a believer living in a secular society?

How should I pray?

How can I forgive someone who is not asking for forgiveness?

If we're trying to decide what car to purchase, what city to move to, what person to marry, what bank to do business with, when to move on to a different job, we will not find specific passages that give pat answers. But such decisions will be easier if we have internalized a broad-based value system from Scripture, which can be applied with intelligence and prayerful dependence. But we won't find a single verse that tells us which way God wants us to go. That is simply not the purpose of Scripture.

Often the questions we ask get reshaped as we go looking for the answers. We realize we have not been asking exactly the right thing. For instance, one of our most common questions is: *How can I know the will of God for my life?* Using a concordance or an online resource, we can go looking for the phrase "will of God." What we will find is that the idea of "the will of God" virtually always relates to the moral quality of our lives. 1 Thessalonians 4:3 is typical: "For this is the will of God, your sanctification" (ESV). This implies that we do not need to go through every decision of every day wondering what the will of God is. "God's will," as Scripture uses the phrase, has nothing to do with deciding between a two-door or four-door car, or getting a family pet, or what classes you sign up for in college. In such matters there are good choices and bad choices, and so we ask God for wisdom, but our study of the idea of "the will of God" in Scripture reframes the very idea of God's will. So we reframe the question itself.

Whenever we are considering a big idea or ideal in Scripture, one that can shape the course of our decisions, it is well worth looking at the idea from numerous angles.

And so we have these two approaches: studying the Bible and taking it as it comes, and searching for answers to life's important questions. In both approaches, we study Scripture as an act of obedience and submission.

In order to do the second, we need to know how to do a thematic or topical study of Scripture, the subject we come to next.

Chapter 16

HOW TO DO A TOPICAL
STUDY OF SCRIPTURE

W hen my children were young, my wife and I tried
to go as a family to a different national park every
summer. My wife and I had not traveled when we
were growing up, so these trips were first-time discoveries for four eager sets of eyes: in the back of the car,
our two children; in the front, the older children, my
wife and I.

Here are two ways of exploring the treasures of a
national park: you can drive through and discover
whatever wonderful things come along the way, taking
a hike here and there, perhaps. Or you can go looking
for something specific—as, on our family trip, we went
looking for waterfalls, mountain peaks, and (for my
wife) birds and wildflowers.

Sometimes we read the Bible progressively, driving through the landscape, discovering its perspective of world history, its chronicles of catastrophes, its spiritual principles. Other times we go looking for specific themes or topics.

So how do we do a thematic or topical study of Scripture? How do we find between the front cover and the back cover the Bible's key teachings on particular topics which can form a cohesive picture of reality?

There are different ways to go about this process, but for now let's look at these five steps: 1) finding the passages; 2) comprehending the topic in context; 3) comparing the various settings; 4) synthesizing the core concepts; and 5) drawing conclusions.

Let's use a topical study of baptism as an example.

1. *Finding the passages.* Here we want to find and make note of the biblical references to our topic, baptism. In this case, we can search for the word "baptism" in a concordance or in a digital search function at a site like Biblegateway.com. In the NIV, we find 21 uses of the word "baptism." But we also need to consider other forms of the word, like "baptize," which yields 50 verses. We can then make a list of all the passages we aim to study, filtering out those which, at a glance, appear not to get at the core meaning of baptism.

2. *Comprehending the topic in context.* If you're exploring a national park for its waterfalls, you don't just

find them, take a quick glance, and then get in the car and drive off. You study each one, walking around, sitting in the mist, closing your eyes and listening to the roar of water. Similarly, it is not enough to merely find the passages related to a given topic and then move on. Once found, you have to linger in them and comprehend their meaning in context. "Baptism" appears in Romans 6:4, but you're not truly engaged in a topical study if you only read that single verse; you have to read the verses around it as well, probably the whole chapter or more. Then you make some provisional conclusions about the meaning of baptism in that particular passage. You make some notes. You go on in this way, passage by passage, noticing repeated ideas, comparisons, contrasts, and explanations.

3. *Comparing the various settings.* Once you have looked up the list of passages and tried your best to understand the meaning in context, you now compare the idea in the various settings. You note where "baptism" refers to the use of water in association with conversion and faith, distinguishing this from the passages where "baptism" is used figuratively.

4. *Synthesizing the core concepts.* To synthesize is to put ideas together. This is Bible study at its highest form. This is where we exercise deep and prayerful thought, taking our time, looking for flashes of insight that reveal connections we never noticed before. Here is where we cluster passages according to type. "Bap-

tism" mentioned in the book of Acts is very important to our understanding because it describes what happened in the early Christian community, while the cluster of passages in the epistles are valuable because they unveil the theology of baptism. Synthesis means comparing passages in similar contexts. At this step, we make more notes, this time about the sub-themes of the topic. We note repeated concepts, and determine which ideas come up only once and will not figure centrally into our conclusions (for instance, "baptize for the dead" in 1 Cor. 15:29). This step should enthuse us. A clearer picture is emerging, and we are able to say, "I never saw that before." This is the glory of synthesis.

5. *Drawing conclusions*. When you begin a topical study, you have some kind of question. It could be, "What does baptism mean?" or "How did first-generation believers practice baptism?" or "What is the enduring theology of baptism?" Your conclusions are your answers to these questions.

Getting clarity on the big ideas of Scripture, especially as we look at the Bible from cover to cover, is a deeply satisfying and faith-building exercise. Often we may feel like getting answers to one question raises all kinds of other questions, but that isn't a problem—it shows that discovering the truth of God is a life-long journey.

Chapter 17

USING BIBLE COMMENTARIES

One day God prompted the apostle Philip to approach an Ethiopian dignitary riding in a chariot along a desert road (Acts 8). The dignitary was reading aloud from the prophet Isaiah, and Philip asked, "Do you understand what you are reading?" The response: "How can I, unless someone explains it to me?"

The man happened to have been reading one of the great prophecies about the coming of Christ and his suffering, and Philip had the privilege of telling the Ethiopian official the good news about Jesus. In that moment, Philip was a kind of commentary for a man who simply needed help with the historical and linguistic meanings of the text of Isaiah.

Serious Bible study will always involve turning to commentaries for guidance and insight. There are different types of commentaries for different purposes, and we ought to use these essential tools at select times in the process of study. This takes nothing away from the principle that the individual believer should be able to read the Bible in a natural and sensible way and derive direct understanding of the text. The reading, understanding, and application of biblical truth have always been functions of the Christian community. The words of the prophets and apostles were directed at God's people (plural) at the start, and must be a community endeavor now. That is why we do personal Bible study, but also engage with others in Bible studies in homes and office buildings and schools and churches.

A Bible commentary is an explanation of the biblical text by someone (usually a scholar) who has immersed himself or herself in the language, context, and form of biblical texts. The Bible commentator delivers information that we simply don't have by the simple reading of Scripture, like archaeological discoveries, historical facts, linguistic particularities, and details about geography and culture.

What kind of commentary should you use? That depends on your purpose. Here are some different types of commentaries:

1. *Critical, technical, and exegetical commentaries* are the most detailed. They exhaustively go through all the details, including comments on the Hebrew, Aramaic,

and Greek words of the text. They are best used by people who know the biblical languages.

2. *Expository commentaries* are written to help people who regularly teach or preach from Scripture, though they are very helpful for any serious student of the Bible. They go passage by passage, sentence by sentence, explaining the background and meaning, but expository commentaries go one step further, describing how the meaning of the text may be applied in life.

3. *Devotional commentaries* spend little time on the details of biblical passages and instead go straight to spiritual meaning and life application.

Note also that there is a big difference between one-volume commentaries on the whole Bible, which are naturally limited, and commentaries devoted to a single book which have much more detail.

When we're doing in-depth study of biblical passages, we should read two or three or more commentaries, making notes as we read. We will quickly see where the commentators agree on the meaning and emphases of texts, and we will gather numerous details not obvious in the simple reading of the text. When it comes to choosing which specific commentaries to use, we note the type of commentary suited for our purpose (above). Then we should note the theological assumptions of the commentators. Some scholars look at the Bible simply as one more human text, and they analyze it in purely linguistic and historical terms. On the other hand, scholars who believe in the divine inspiration and unique character of Scripture will take events like miracles and the resurrection of Christ as historical realities, and will look for the cohesive themes of the revelation of God in Holy Scripture. Commentaries in the evangelical tradition, for instance, are produced by the mainstream evangelical publishers: Baker, Zondervan, InterVarsity Press, and many others.

When the Ethiopian in the chariot said, "How can I understand, unless someone explains it to me?" he displayed the curiosity and teachability that is essential for all followers of Jesus. We are blessed today with many experts who have done diligent study to help us as we search for the meaning of the Scriptures.

[See the list of recommended commentaries at www.WordWay.org/HowToStudyTheBible.]

Chapter 18

STUDYING A BIBLICAL CHARACTER

The core meaning of the Bible is easy to discern when we simply read it from cover to cover. The core meaning is centered on God and people, and God's action to save a broken people. In this, Scripture is like a great drama with one main character, God, and multitudes of supporting characters. Thousands of named characters, in fact. Some are only names in long genealogies, others are the subjects of epic narratives. Abraham, Joseph, Moses, Peter, Paul, and Jesus, to name a few. Scripture contains truth, of course, but the truth is incarnate in God himself and in the real-life stories of the people God moved.

So it is no surprise that, in Bible study, we want to occasionally do a character study. By character we mean the biography of a real person, and the inner qualities that made him or her great or evil, or both.

How do we study a biblical character?

First, we need to start with the right assumptions. Remember that a narrative passage of Scripture tells us truthfully what people did and said, and occasionally interprets their lives. The story of Abraham is told from Genesis 11 through 25 in great detail. We learn about his origins in Ur, his coming to Canaan, God's promise to him, his sojourn in the land, his dealings with allies and enemies, his family relationships, and his interactions with God. From this account we get many profound insights on human nature and the ways of God. Abraham was, and is, the father of faith. But not all the details in Abraham's story have a parallel in our lives. There are lessons in the near-sacrifice of Isaac, and the life of the Bedouin shepherd, and the struggle of faith, but we should not strain to apply the details of Abraham's life to our own lives because the story of Abraham is the story of Abraham.

Also, though a heroic figure, not everything Abraham did was righteous. A "hero" in any biblical narrative is still a flawed and sinful human being—including Abraham, Jacob, Moses, David, Peter, and Paul. The narratives about the lives of major figures in Scripture give us a few guiding spiritual principles, rather than lessons in every small detail. We must not lose the forest for the trees. From Abraham we get the lesson of faith "counted as righteousness" by God. We also get a picture of hope. As Hebrews 11 says, Abraham and other heroes of the faith often went to the end of their lives without seeing what they were promised.

Second, we need to find the right passages. If you want to do a character study of Barnabas, for instance, you can easily find the 33 passages where the name comes up by using a concordance or an online tool like Biblegateway.com. But you need to make sure all the passages in the list refer to the same person. In the New Testament, for instance, there are numerous people named Mary, James, and John. The context of the passages will usually be all the guidance you need to focus on a single person.

Third, we need to read each of the passages, in context. Just reading isolated verses will not do, because we need context to understand every reference to a character. We read the verses around the reference, or perhaps a whole chapter, making notes on what we observe along the way. Our observations may include:

- the circumstances of the narrative
- how the person behaved or spoke
- the rightness or wrongness in what he or she did
- the awareness the person had of God's truth and righteousness
- the growth or decline of the character across the narrative

This last part is extremely important. Character development is often where we find the profound truths of a person's life. Getting insight into Saul of Tarsus who became Paul the Apostle, for instance, is central to his significance. We have enough information to learn about his motivations and not just his actions (and, in Paul's case, we are helped by what he says in his epistles). Studying the character of Judas may not seem like a high priority, but when you read the passages where he is mentioned carefully and progressively, a fascinating picture emerges of an ordinary man who gradually became confused and dark. We need to understand where a Judas went wrong.

Fourth, we need to draw conclusions and make applications. It may be helpful to think about the essence of the person's life. What is the big picture of his or her story, and are there parallels with our lives today? Some characters yield few lessons, if any, and we should not force the issue. But others are intended to be models for us. Hebrews 11, for instance, mentions Abraham, Isaac, Jacob, Moses, Rahab, Gideon, Samson, David, Samuel, and others, all as illustrations of this singular, powerful lesson: "These were all commended for their faith, yet none of them received what had been promised, since God had planned something better for us so that only together with us would they be made perfect" (vss. 39-40).

Biography has always been a strong literary form in any context. In the many genres of Scripture, we have the full and partial biographies of hundreds of real-life characters. Sometimes we just have a few details about a character's life, but there is enough there for us to derive powerful lessons. And though we need to be careful to sort out the virtuous details of a biblical character from his or her flaws, we also have compelling examples for us to emulate.

Part III

INTERPRETING AND APPLYING THE BIBLE

Chapter 19

THE BASICS OF BIBLE
INTERPRETATION

Some people believe that because there have been so
many different interpretations of the Bible over the centuries it's almost hopeless to get at its actual meaning.
Nothing could be further from the truth. While there
will always be small details in the biblical text that
seem elusive, the basic meaning of the Bible, passage
by passage, is accessible to us all. Think of it this way:
when Paul wrote a letter to a group of believers, he
meant something specific and he wanted to be understood. So also with David writing a Psalm or Jeremiah
speaking an oracle or the writer of Chronicles giving a
timeline or Luke giving his "orderly account" of the
life and ministry of Jesus. And if the Bible is the word
of God, we can also assume this: God wants to be un-

derstood. God has graced us with wisdom and guidance, with confrontation and warning, with love and hope—all delivered through the words of the prophets and apostles.

There are a few basic principles of Bible interpretation. If we can hold these ideas in our heads when we read Scripture, most of what we read will be clear.

1. *The simplest and most natural explanation of a Biblical text is always the best.* This is how your friend expects you to read and understand a letter or an email, and this is what the writers of Scripture expected when they wrote. If the text says that Jesus and his disciples traveled from Galilee to Jerusalem, that is exactly what is meant.

2. *The Bible is its own best interpreter.* Most of the expressions in Scripture that seem challenging or mysterious have probably appeared in Scripture elsewhere. We therefore look up and cross reference these instances, and the meaning becomes clear. This is especially true of large, expansive themes. Want to know the meaning of salvation, or sin, or Messiah, or marriage, or church? Then understand the passage you are looking at in the context of the whole of what the Bible itself says, more so than any external sources.

3. *Recognize how figurative and literal language works.* The metaphors, similes, parables, and symbols of Scripture are powerful ways the writers communicated. When Jesus said he was the "door" of the sheep-

fold, he gave us a memorable figurative expression of his protection. Symbolic and figurative language is not inferior to the literal. Take an expression as literal when the natural way of reading the text is to take the words in their usual sense. Jesus is not literally a door, but when in John 20 it says that the disciples were gathered behind locked doors, we take door there in its normal literal sense. Unfortunately, sometimes today we use the word *literal* to mean "really" or "truly," which is not what the word *literal* has historically meant, and it causes confusion. If someone says, "It's literally raining cats and dogs outside," he or she does not mean pets are dropping from the sky. So yes, we take the Bible to be literal where its language is meant to be literal, but figurative where the biblical authors intended to be figurative or symbolic. One is not superior to the other.

5. *The methods we use to interpret the Bible are basically the same as those we use to interpret any written text.* We get at the meaning of words, the way words work together, the background of the texts, the historical setting of the text, etc.—just as we would when studying any kind of written communication. The outcome in this case is the life-changing word of God, but the way we come to understand it is the same way we interpret written texts in general. (This, by the way, is why ordinary believers can read and understand the Bible for themselves rather than being dependent upon a few enlightened teachers.)

6. *A particular biblical text has a particular meaning.* It may be applied in various ways, but the meaning is specific to the intent of the author. This prohibits us from deciding that biblical texts mean whatever we want them to mean, which is an insult to the intent of God.

7. *The Bible has large controlling themes, and these help us interpret its various parts.* For example, in the Old Testament we find these controlling themes: covenant, promise, the land, the people of God. In the New Testament, the central theme is Jesus the Christ. And from the perspective of the New Testament we understand how the coming Messiah is a central theme in the Old Testament as well.

Interpreting the Bible correctly is the way we respect the biblical authors, revere God, and discover the depth and breadth of biblical truth.

Chapter 20

LET SCRIPTURE INTERPRET SCRIPTURE

When you read a passage and wonder what "resurrection" really means—or "the kingdom of God" or "sexual immorality" or "Passover" or "antichrist" or "marriage"—there is one place to turn: the rest of the Scriptures. Yes, archaeologists may have some relevant information, and there may be parallels in modern literature, science, or history, but Scripture is its own best interpreter.

The New Testament passages about the church are best explained by all the other passages about the church in the New Testament. The Lord's Supper is best interpreted by Jesus' "I am the bread" teaching, and by the meals like Passover in the Old Testament and the manna sent from heaven. Most of the incredible images and numbers from the book of Revelation, over which people puzzle, and which have produced wildly different interpretations going in every possible direction, have already appeared in the Bible before (e.g., the mark on the forehead, a beast rising up out of the sea, the numbers 1,000, 7, 12, etc.). There is a vivid meaning in each instance, and it is amazing how much easier it is to get at if we look up just one or two other passages that use the same language.

The Reformers spoke about "the analogy of faith," which is the idea that Scripture must interpret Scripture, so we compare and synthesize various passages that all speak on the same theme.

Art is about repetition and variation, and so too are history and theology. God gives us a truth like, "I am your Savior," and then repeats it a hundred different ways throughout Scripture. Repetition and variation. The words change slightly, metaphors are used, and through it all—by the words of the prophets and the apostles—God's word comes through strong and clear. We see the form of it all. Its lines become clearer and bolder. Conviction firms up in our minds and hearts.

And this is why we must read Scripture as a rhythmic discipline of our lives. It is a big book. It is full of epic stories, oracles, sermons, prophecies, letters, songs, and proverbs that address the whole of life. It reveals God in all his actions and attributes. The Bible is a vivid mosaic of hundreds of personal stories in which people are trying to find God, or trying to make or be their own god. It explains the issues of the 21st century as precisely as it does any other century. It is our best guide for life. It is the only direct and pure expression of God's own mind.

When we read it as if studying a tapestry, we will be building a comprehensive structure of truth for our lives. We will see the patches of truth emerge and converge into a great patchwork. We'll be able to say, "Oh, that's what joy means!" as we put together the pattern we get from Psalms and Luke and Philippians. We'll be able to say, "I now understand temptation because this passage in James explains what I read a while ago in Romans and in Matthew." We'll know the difference between a major theme that God wants us to understand because it comes up so often (like sanctification, or forgiveness, or sin) and minor themes that should not be our focus (like, "Where was Jesus between his death and resurrection?").

The Bible is God's word to us about himself. It is the speech of a sovereign Lord and loving Father; it is the word about Jesus the Word; it is the breath of the Spirit. This is not about literary criticism. It is an act of grace unfolding in our lives. When we read Scripture, we can pray something like this:

Holy Spirit, you inspired the writers of Scripture. Now please illumine my mind that I may grasp the width, length, height, and depth of your truth and life.

Chapter 21

ILLUMINATION AND THE STUDY
OF SCRIPTURE

The idea of the inspiration of the Scriptures is fairly familiar. This is the conviction that the authors of the Bible were inspired by the Holy Spirit to put down words that had the full truth and authority of the word of God. But there is a corresponding and equally important principle: illumination. This is a core belief that spans the centuries of Christian faith.

To put it succinctly: in inspiration, God the Holy Spirit used the writers of Scripture in order to reveal God's truth; in illumination, God the Holy Spirit enlivens the minds of the readers of Scripture so that they may understand what God has put there.

This is what Paul prayed for when he said:

I keep asking that the God of our Lord Jesus Christ, the glorious Father, may give you the Spirit of wisdom and revelation, so that you may know him better. I pray that the eyes of your heart may be enlightened in order that you may know the hope to which he has called you, the riches of his glorious inheritance in his holy people (Eph. 1:17-18).

Most of Psalm 119 (the longest of the Psalms) is a prayer seeking understanding of God's will, ways, and word. For instance, verse 34: "Give me understanding, so that I may keep your law and obey it with all my heart."

When we study the Bible we use all the normal methods we use to understand any text: the history, the grammar, the words, etc. But believers do not stop there. We know that the truth of God which exceeds human understanding requires a work of the Holy Spirit in order for us to comprehend it.

This is why it is wise to pray before and after we read Scripture. Here, for instance, are two prayers as examples:

Before Reading the Bible

Open my eyes, gracious Lord, as I turn to your word. I long to know you, to understand life, and to be changed. Examine me, Lord, by the floodlight of your truth. Amen.

After Reading the Bible

May the word I have read, Lord, be planted deeply in my mind and heart. Help me not to walk away and forget it, but to meditate on it and obey it and so build my life on the rock of your truth. Amen.

This is another reason for us to read Scripture thoughtfully, without distraction, and at times when we are able to walk away and reflect on what we've read. In our hurried lives we often miss the all-important discipline of meditation. When we pause and reflect, the Holy Spirit does the work of illumination.

Chapter 22

ONE MEANING,
MANY APPLICATIONS

The world is a better place when millions of Christians study the Bible seriously, searching hard for the original meaning of its authors, uncovering the foundations on which all of life can be based. But the world is not a better place when those students of the Bible neglect to apply the truth of Scripture to real life, accurately and faithfully.

There was a group of people in Jesus' time who prided themselves on studying the Scriptures, but their application of it was selfish and skewed. We know them as the Pharisees and Sadducees and "teachers of the law." One day when Jesus confronted them over their interpretation of the Scriptures, he said, "You are in error because you do not know the Scriptures or the power of God" (Matt. 22:29). A shocking statement, to be sure.

Knowing the Scriptures means careful reading, observation, analysis, and background checking, followed by application of the meaning of Scripture to our lives.

Here is an extremely important principle: a particular biblical passage has a singular and specific meaning—that is, it does not have many different meanings. But a particular biblical passage does have multiple valid applications.

For example, James 1:19-20 says, "My dear brothers and sisters, take note of this: Everyone should be quick to listen, slow to speak and slow to become angry, because human anger does not produce the righteousness that God desires."

We study this passage to get at the specific and singular meaning. We note that this injunction is similar to Proverbs in the Old Testament (which is true of much of the book of James). It is not directed at one particular group of people, as might be the case in a book like 1 Corinthians or 1 Timothy; it is a principle of healthy living for all believers. We look at key words like "listen" and "angry" and "anger." We conclude that this passage is a general exhortation to believers that we should listen more and react less. Especially, we should restrain any knee-jerk reactions of anger.

Once we've done a careful reading, we apply the singular meaning of that passage to our own lives. The application goes to many different real-life situations, and validly so.

• Husbands and wives should take the effort to really listen to each other, which may mean asking back and forth for clarification, rather than reacting in anger, which erodes a marriage.

• When people respond negatively to a Christian leader's decisions, the leader should listen carefully, seeking to understand and even to acknowledge the validity of at least a portion of the objection. Above all, the leader should not react in anger.

• When a believer is confronted by a co-worker, it can be good Christian witness to listen to the confrontation, try to understand what it means, and to honestly engage the critic.

• A parent whose kid is upset can choose to take the time to understand what exactly is going on rather than just adding fuel to the fire.

The applications of James' "quick to listen... slow to speak... slow to become angry" can go on and on. And that's what's exciting about studying and applying the Scriptures. When we study the Bible, we are acting as objective analysts, committing ourselves to getting at the objective meaning that the prophets and apostles intended to convey. We do so out of respect for the authors, and, even more, out of respect for God. Once we get the meaning, we enthusiastically seek to apply it to as many different life situations as we can.

Jesus did not want his listeners to merely debate his meaning. He wanted his teaching to shape their lives. That is why he said:

"Therefore everyone who hears these words of mine and puts them into practice is like a wise man who built his house on the rock. The rain came down, the streams rose, and the winds blew and beat against that house; yet it did not fall, because it had its foundation on the rock. But everyone who hears these words of mine and does not put them into practice is like a foolish man who built his house on sand. The rain came down, the streams rose, and the winds blew and beat against that house, and it fell with a great crash" (Matt. 7:24-27).

And it is why James said:

"Do not merely listen to the word, and so deceive yourselves. Do what it says. Anyone who listens to the word but does not do what it says is like someone who looks at his face in a mirror and, after looking at himself, goes away and immediately forgets what he looks like. But whoever looks intently into the perfect law that gives freedom, and continues in it—not forgetting what they have heard, but doing it—they will be blessed in what they do" (James 1:22-25).

We study the Scriptures not to gain some special, secret knowledge. We study the Scriptures in order for our lives to be confronted, challenged, and transformed.

Chapter 23

THE INDWELLING WORD

I love being around people who have so deeply taken the word of God into their lives that it has shaped the very way they think, their overall attitude toward life, their reactions to minor and major events, even their temperament. This is the fruit, developed by the Holy Spirit, of love, joy, peace, patience, kindness, goodness, gentleness, faithfulness, and self-control. These are the signs that the word of God has truly become lodged into the deepest part of who they are–into the heart, where opinions are formed and motives are birthed, where emotions are sparked and decisions are set.

These are not people who look to impress others by quoting Scripture all the time, or who feel obligated to slap a verse on every event of life. They so respect Scripture that they avoid twisting it to suit their purposes. The Bible is never a weapon in their hands, nor merely a tool. It is more than an encyclopedia of spiritual knowledge. It is the voice of God—sometimes a whisper, sometimes a shout, but always a revelation of God's own pure character. It is thus the wisdom of God, the power of God, the love of God, the light of God, the truth of God. These humbly righteous people read the Bible because they long to know God and to have a God-filled life.

But how does the word of God get firmly planted in us?

Whenever I have come upon Colossians 3:16, which says, "Let the word of Christ dwell in you richly," it has always challenged, enthused, and comforted me. "Dwell in you richly." Of course that's what God wants! I'm not a computer hard drive whose purpose is to collect more and more data. I'm not a student hoping against hope to get all the answers right on the final exam. I'm a member of God's household, and I get to learn God's word with my brothers and sisters, and to ask God to make that word go down deeply and effectively, down to a place where it won't get blown away by the winds of today's concerns. I can ask God to make it take root, so that it will dwell there and nobody will be able to take it away. And it will not lie dormant. It will, like well-planted seed, sprout and grow and put down roots, and finally, as it grows and matures, it will be ready for harvesting and digesting. We take it in as seed, but it becomes a nourishing feast.

Colossians 3:16 also says that there are a variety of ways the word of Christ goes deep enough to dwell. Teaching is paramount, so we need to keep searching like eagles for teachers, authors, and Bible study leaders who explain and apply the word faithfully. "Admonishing with wisdom" suggests a flow of quality conversation among believers about what they are learning from God. "Singing praise" is another powerful way the word of God is carried deeply into our hearts. Singing "with gratitude in [our] hearts to God" can crack open the crusty and hardened exterior of our lives. Seeds drop deeply in, and they begin to live and grow.

Why sing? So the word will dwell richly. Why a variety of sounds (psalms, hymns, spiritual songs)? So the word will knock on the doors of our hearts, every door that is the least bit cracked open. Why teach? So that the word will be clearly explained and powerfully applied. Worship is not the span of time between the beginning and the end of singing; it is this great and varied advance of the word on our souls.

And then there is meditation—a way of reading Scripture in such a way that it has a chance to get planted. Meditation is a word that the Bible uses to describe a way of holding and pondering God's truth so that it sinks in. It is wise, pensive concentration.

At the edge of the promised land, Joshua told the people they were going to need real spiritual muscle. Wars lay ahead. Three times at the Jordan River, he said, "Be strong and courageous," and then: "Do not let this Book of the Law depart from your mouth; meditate on it day and night, so that you may be careful to do everything written in it. Then you will be prosperous and successful."

The Psalms speak about meditating on the word of God, and continuing that meditation through every pulse of life. Psalm 119 describes a committed discipline of taking the word in:

"I meditate on your precepts and consider your ways" (vs. 15). "Though rulers sit together and slander me, your servant will meditate on your decrees" (vs. 23).

"Let me understand the teaching of your precepts; then I will meditate on your wonders" (vs. 27).

"I lift up my hands to your commands, which I love, and I meditate on your decrees" (vs. 48).

"May the arrogant be put to shame for wronging me without cause; but I will meditate on your precepts" (vs. 78).

"Oh, how I love your law! I meditate on it all day long" (vs. 97).

"I have more insight than all my teachers, for I meditate on your statutes" (vs. 99).

The way I look at people who have had a pattern of Scripture digestion over the years is that the word which they consume faithfully is transformed into the spiritual muscle tissue of their lives. The word of God becomes part of who they are.

These people do not view Scripture as a collection of magical sayings which work wonders when voiced. They consistently act out of the truth of Scripture. Their reactions to people around them are governed by patience and gentleness because they have a graduate degree in grace, as it were (in learning and in experience). They react with truth because their consciences have been trained and shaped to stay within the bounds of honest, authentic reality. Their instincts, which are as naturally fallen as any of ours, have been retrained. They don't even think: "What is the biblical thing to do or say?" because biblical ethics and ethos have become essential to who they are. This is what was promised in the new covenant when God said, "I will put my law in their minds, and write it on their hearts" (Jeremiah 31:33).

Chapter 24

AVOIDING MISTAKES IN THE APPLICATION OF SCRIPTURE

I always feel a little insulted when I read the instructions on a tube of antiseptic ointment: APPLY TOPI-CALLY. NOT TO BE INGESTED. I figure that much is obvious. But there would be a real problem, of course, if someone were to swallow a medicine that was supposed to be applied to the skin.

Application is the last step in the so-called inductive method of Bible study. ("Inductive" means drawing general conclusions from particular observations. "Inductive Bible study" goes from observation to interpretation to application.)

The first step is to *observe* (examining the words, the structure, the details), the second step is to *interpret* (figuring out what the author meant), and then finally, *application* (figuring out how the truths we uncover connect with everyday life). We know that if our observation is incomplete or our interpretation is askew, we will miss the truth and power of Scripture. But it is also true that misapplication of the meaning of biblical texts is invalid and even dangerous.

Here are some of the most common mistakes to avoid when applying Scripture:

1. *Imagining a spiritual meaning that is not embedded in the text itself.*

Narrative texts—whether they are the stories of the Old Testament historical books, or the four Gospels, or the book of Acts—mostly describe the unfolding of real-life stories. We gain lessons about life from these stories, but usually there is not a simple "moral to the story" unless indicated by the text itself. The way God guided the Israelites through the wilderness is not the way he guides you or me to a job opportunity. The military tactics of Joshua are best understood as a description of what happened, not as a strategy for successful living. The transfiguration of Jesus on the mountain was a unique historic event. Its significance is about the identity of Jesus, and does not really have a parallel in my life. Narrative texts have meaning in the context of the whole sweeping story of the people of God. But their details may be applied only when clearly indicated or there is a transcendent principle like Joshua telling the people "choose this day whom you will serve" (Joshua 24:15).

2. *Taking historical narratives as prescriptive rather than descriptive.*

Narratives tell us what happened; they don't necessarily tell us what should have happened, or what should happen today in our lives. For example, we glean from the book of Acts how the first generation of Christians lived, but that does not prescribe how we should live. Acts 2:46 says the first believers met every day in the temple courts. That does not mean that believers today are obligated to gather every day in one specific place. They sold their property and gave the proceeds away—an example of generous, open hearts, but not a command that believers must adopt socialist politics. We know that in the first century churches were led by elders, sometimes supervised by an apostle or an apostle's representative, like Timothy. Later in the New Testament, the role of deacons was developed. But this does not mean it's wrong today for a church to have new designated roles, like a senior pastor, or pastors of children or evangelism or worship, or small group leaders.

3. *Using an application that is not connected with the actual meaning of the text.*

Jesus' statement, "I am the bread of life" (John 6:35, 48, 51), is not about physical nutrition. "Let us run with perseverance the race marked out for us" (Heb. 12:1) is not about competing with your co-workers or neighbors—it is about perseverance, as is directly stated in the text. Paul saying, "I have become all things to all people" (1 Cor. 9:22) does not mean we should conform ourselves to our parents' expectations in order to get along.

It is possible to take any Scripture text and use the words as a springboard to leap to any meaning our whim chooses. And we need to be aware of this: sadly, many sermons given in many of our churches do exactly that. It is very easy for teachers and pastors to have preconceived ideas about what they want to say, and then go looking for biblical texts that have some merely verbal connection. To use its words disconnected from their original meaning is an abuse of Scripture, and it's an insult to God's intention.

4. *Reading your own theology into the text.*

If someone has strong convictions about sexual ethics, that's good, but it is a mistake to see immorality wherever there is a mention of sin in the Bible. Someone else may really like the doctrine of grace, but tend to underplay the corresponding principle of truth. Grace is amazing, it really is, and it appears throughout Scripture, including in words like mercy, love, and benevolence. But grace is balanced by truth. Likewise, someone who loves to proclaim truth must not leave grace behind.

It is hard for us to see what our theological presuppositions are, but if we do not, we will frequently apply Scripture in unbalanced ways, and we will be less likely to have the joy of discovering truths we had not seen before.

Applying Scripture is the reward of study well done. But we need to make sure we're applying the truth exactly where it belongs.

Chapter 25

DEVOTIONAL REFLECTION

In a devotional study of a passage, we are focusing on *reflection*. We might think of reflection as what we do between detailed study of the meaning of a passage (exegesis) and application. Reflection is an intentional process of letting the powerful meaning of a passage sink in. If we are looking at a narrative passage (see the examples below), we are using some mental energy to place ourselves in the original context, trying to understand what the original participants might have been experiencing. We must be careful to not be overly speculative, but it is okay to wonder what Mary Magdalene or Peter or Jeremiah might have been thinking or seeing or feeling in their particular contexts. Reflection is a way for us to close the chronological gap (thousands of years) and the cultural gap that we always have with the text of Scripture. It is also a way for us to realize in an immediate way how the passage might apply to us.

What follows are two excerpts from my devotional, *Knowing Him: Devotional Readings about the Cross and Resurrection.*

* * *

THE CRUCIFIXION

They came to a place called Golgotha (which means "the place of the skull"). There they offered Jesus wine to drink, mixed with gall; but after tasting it, he refused to drink it. When they had crucified him, they divided up his clothes by casting lots. And sitting down, they kept watch over him there. Above his head they placed the written charge against him: THIS IS JESUS, THE KING OF THE JEWS. — Matthew 27:33-37

Now came the time for the clash between good and evil, heaven and hell. The crucifixion of Jesus is both the most horrific moment in human history, and humanity's only hope. That's why we call the Friday before Easter, Good Friday.

Jesus' followers were still too weak to understand, and so they scattered. The religious elite carried out their plot. The political leaders passed the buck, and in the end, they discarded Jesus for the sake of convenience. The crowds gawked. Two thieves hung on either side of a man whose crime was hard to comprehend. The placard above his head announced with biting sarcasm: King of the Jews. That must have attracted some attention.

We know of seven things Jesus said from that cross, including a pronouncement of forgiveness for the soldiers, provision for the care of his mother, and a plea for something to wet his parched mouth. But the last words on that last day of his natural human life were the most important: "It is finished!" (John 19:30). That was not a cry of resignation, nor capitulation or surrender. It was a shout of victory that all that God had planned for the restoration of sinful human beings was now accomplished. Now there could be justification! Redemption! Reconciliation! All that needed to be done for the debt and scar of sin had been done. Forgiveness was now free.

All that remained was for Jesus to step out from the shadow of death, which he would easily do after a few days. But first, the disciples had time to search their hearts for how something good could be found in something so bad. And the enemies of God disappeared into the darkness of their own duplicity.

Ponder this: How does the crucifixion of Jesus most powerfully impact you?

* * * * *

THE RESURRECTION

Early on the first day of the week, while it was still dark, Mary Magdalene went to the tomb and saw that the stone had been removed from the entrance. So she came running to Simon Peter and the other disciple, the one Jesus loved, and said, "They have taken the Lord out of the tomb, and we don't know where they have put him!" — John 20:1-2

How difficult was it for the One who is Lord of the universe—who had a hand in creation itself, who is the very force of life that holds living things together—to wake up from the sleep of death and set aside the burial cloths draping his body?

As was always the case, Jesus' revelations of himself did not happen with television cameras focused on him. Not even a respectable crowd was gathered. An alarming word from young Mary Magdalene about Jesus' body being gone produced a panic and a footrace among two of Jesus' beloved disciples, Peter and John. One looked and merely saw the emptiness of the tomb; the other saw the connection between this moment and the mysterious words of Jesus—and he believed.

Now things were really complicated and the disciples went home. So Jesus first appeared to a brokenhearted Mary who stayed at the tomb. Mary was the first to behold something the world had never seen before—a resurrected, transformed life.

Resurrection day for Jesus was simply the first installment of a resurrection of masses of people when this era of the history of the universe draws to a close. What God promises to those who belong to Jesus is not the loss of self into a nothingness bliss, but the resurrection and remaking of everything that is right and good in the world he created. And until then, he invites us to begin living transformed lives, continually shaped and changed by the hope of the redemption of all that God has made.

Ponder this: Where in your life do you need the resurrection power of Jesus at work today?

Chapter 26

HOW TO RECOGNIZE
FALSE TEACHING

When I was young in the faith, I had a deep hunger to find the truth of God because I had tasted it, and it was deeply satisfying. I sensed that my soul was just waiting to be revived from some kind of hibernation. I sought out different Christian teachers and preachers, read some best-selling books, and sampled Christian radio teaching. But I was unsettled by the feeling that the Bible teaching I heard seemed sometimes only loosely linked with the biblical text—it was peculiar, out of sync. It didn't have the "ring of truth" I experienced when reading Scripture itself.

Some years later, I came to the conclusion that the "smell test" needs to be taken seriously: if we are exposed to teaching that just doesn't "smell" right, then we ought to proceed carefully. Maybe the teaching is sound and we just need to get in sync with it, or it may be that our senses are all right, and we're hearing that most dangerous thing—false teaching.

The Bible itself speaks of false teaching. There is a difference between truth and falsehood, and when it comes to Bible interpretation, a lot of what we hear is garbage—and it smells that way.

How do we guard ourselves against false teaching?

First, we need to watch out for opportunists. Teachers who gain illicitly from their teaching need to be avoided. It is amazing how many masses of people will follow manipulative, grossly greedy, and dishonest "teachers." They promise prosperity if others make them prosperous, and they laugh all the way to the bank. The short epistle of Jude offers a stark analysis of this kind of false teacher:

"These people are blemishes at your love feasts, eating with you without the slightest qualm—shepherds who feed only themselves. They are clouds without rain, blown along by the wind; autumn trees, without fruit and uprooted—twice dead. They are wild waves of the sea, foaming up their shame; wandering stars, for whom blackest darkness has been reserved forever. ... These people are grumblers and faultfinders; they follow their own evil desires; they boast about themselves and flatter others for their own advantage" (Jude 12-13, 16).

This is a stunning description of the destructive effects of "shepherds who feed only themselves." The passage indicates that we must watch out for the selfishness, fruitlessness, chaos, and arrogance of certain people. They gain influence through their sheer conceit. Ironically, we give them credence on the basis of their pride, the character flaw that most disqualifies them. When we realize we have been sucked in by this kind of false teacher, we need to do some soul-searching to figure out why.

A second kind of false teaching is ill-founded speculation. Some people make a career of spouting out details on topics like spiritual life or end-times prophesy or cosmology, which go way beyond what Scripture actually teaches. Speculation delivers chaos, not meaning. Sometimes the motive is manipulation—esoteric knowledge can be a power tactic. The last sentence of 1 Timothy is this plea:

"O Timothy, guard the deposit entrusted to you. Avoid the irreverent babble and contradictions of what is falsely called 'knowledge,' for by professing it some have swerved from the faith" (1 Tim. 6:20-21 ESV).

Second Timothy contains a similar warning:

"Charge them before God not to quarrel about words, which does no good, but only ruins the hearers. Do your best to present yourself to God as one approved, a worker who has no need to be ashamed, rightly handling the word of truth. But avoid irreverent babble, for it will lead people into more and more un-godliness, and their talk will spread like gangrene" (2 Tim. 2:14-17 ESV).

A third kind of false teaching is legalism. Jesus confronted this distortion of God's truth when he exposed the corrupt side of sectarianism: "Woe to you Pharisees, because you give God a tenth of your mint, rue and all other kinds of garden herbs, but you neglect justice and the love of God" (Luke 11:42). First Timothy 4:3 warns about teachers who "forbid people to marry and order them to abstain from certain foods, which God created to be received with thanksgiving by those who believe and who know the truth."

These and other forms of false teaching all have causes, and we will avoid spiritual collisions if we see them ahead of time. False teaching can come from naiveté, arrogance, or selfish gain. The problem we face today is that it isn't hard to grab a microphone, create a webpage, or self-publish a book. We must make careful choices about whom we listen to, and we must have the strength to turn away when a suspicious teacher is tickling our ears and offering false comfort.

[This chapter is an excerpt from *How to Understand the Bible: A Simple Guide* WordWay, 2014.]

Chapter 27

WE ARE IN THIS TOGETHER

Let's imagine ourselves as believers in first century Thessalonica, Greece, the day the leaders of the church received a letter—a letter from the founder of the church, the apostle Paul.

You are one of the elders of the church, and you read Paul's instructions and admonitions with a sense of urgency and care. There is no "New Testament" as the 27 books we know today. The Gospels have not been written yet, nor Romans or Hebrews or Revelation. You and the rest of the leaders in Thessalonica are following the gradually unfolding apostolic teaching which formed the foundation of the early church (Ephesians 2:20). You listen carefully to the words, read out loud by one of the other elders.

And then an important process unfolds. You discuss with your fellow church leaders what you have just heard from Paul. You go over what he has written about suffering and sanctification and salvation. You ask for someone to re-read the bit about the coming of Christ. Someone suggests the entire letter be read again, from the beginning.

You discuss Paul's points. Sometimes there is a little disagreement over something specific Paul said. You talk about why he wanted this church, the believers in Thessalonica, to understand these specific things.

You consider how to apply the meaning of Paul's words. A leader suggests one application, and someone else enthusiastically suggests another. After a couple hours of discussion, you realize that this short letter, this authoritative word from God's chosen apostle, is going to reverberate in your community for a long time to come. Paul has addressed some controversies, reinforced some teachings, and pioneered new ideas.

You come to understand this letter to the Christian community in your city of Thessalonica because you have read it together, discussed it together, and applied it together.

So here we are in the 21st century, reading the same words, attempting to get the meaning and apply it responsibly and fully. We do so not in isolation, but with other believers. We get the gold from the goldmine of

Scripture not by prospecting in isolation, but by working together.

Bible study is a community effort. For some people, that impulse comes naturally. They don't want to be isolated. They read Scripture and immediately want to compare reactions and interpretations with others. Some people, however, so value that holy time when they privately read and explore Scripture, asking the Holy Spirit for illumination, enthused with new discoveries, slain by confrontation, inspired by new visions of God, that they almost want to avoid discussing the Bible with other people. They may believe that private interpretations of Scripture are sacrosanct, and that comparing notes with others takes something away from their genuine interaction with God.

We need to be balanced here. On the one hand, the truth of God in Scripture is available and accessible to any individual believer. No one stands between us and God. But, on the other hand, we are in this together. God gives different insights to different people—not splitting the meaning of his word, but revealing different facets of it. That's the way Scripture functioned in ancient times, and it's the way we should study it today.

What does that look like?

1. *We should all find fine Bible teachers and benefit from their instruction.* That will include local pastors, but there is also good teaching on the radio and the inter-

net. We have a huge advantage today in being able to subscribe to podcasts or log in to sermons preached thousands of miles away. It is better to listen to multiple teachers rather than just one. We are disciples of only one figure—Jesus the Christ—not the pastor with the largest podcast.

2. *We should read widely, but with discernment.* You can Google any Bible question you have and get hundreds of links, but much of what you'll find is junk. Know the writers you follow—their organizations, their publishers, their associations.

3. *We should view our use of commentaries and other tools produced by reliable scholars as a function of the wider Christian community.* In other words, we should not take the distinction between ordinary Bible students and experts as a separation of classes. Are there experts in Bible scholarship? Of course there are. They are the ones who do archaeological digs in the hills of Judea, who study the scrawling script of ancient Greek texts, who can define the meaning of obscure words, etc. They write the Bible dictionaries and commentaries, the atlases and specialized studies. But no one wants to go back to the days of the Pharisees and teachers of the law, or of the passive laity of Europe's Middle Ages. We all get to do our own Bible study. We all must discover the flow of meaning of biblical books and have the joy of finding the gold in the goldmine. Along the way, we benefit from the work of the experts. But we

also assert that the plain meaning of Scripture is available to every believer as surely as God himself is.

4. *We should study Scripture with other believers in our communities.* It is exciting to sit in a circle and work through Bible study when it is led by someone who understands Scripture and knows the proper methods of interpretation. It is powerful when members of the group contribute their observations, ask their questions, explore their thoughts about application. The leader should commit to being well prepared, and facilitate a rational discussion, guiding the group and drawing people out. Group Bible study should not be passive listening, and it should not be a pooling of ignorance. Group Bible study works best when it unfolds over a long period of time.

We are in this together, just like the early communities of believers. The beauty of it is that we get to know God better as we get to know each other better. The truth of Scripture is a living, dynamic force in our lives. On our best days we see that power in us—and we see it in each other.

Chapter 28

CONVICTION AND COMMITMENT

Some of the great Christian leaders of the past based their lives and work on their intimate and deep knowledge of the truth of God in Scripture. Some spoke out forcibly, compelling all believers to take Bible reading and study seriously. Their commitment rose from their deep-seated conviction. Here are a few examples.

Richard Baxter:

Study hard, for the well is deep, and our brains are shallow. But especially be laborious in practice and in the exercise of your knowledge.

Martin Luther:

You cannot read too much in Scripture, what you read you cannot read too carefully, what you read carefully you cannot understand too well, what you understand well you cannot teach too well, what you teach well you cannot live too well... Therefore dear... pastors and preachers, pray, read, study, be diligent... This evil, shameful time is no season for being lazy, for sleeping, and snoring. (The Cambridge Companion to Martin Luther; Donald K. McKim, Cambridge University Press, July 2003).

John Wesley, who here makes six key practical points:

If you desire to read the Scriptures in such a manner as may most effectually answer this end, would it not be advisable,

(1) To set apart a little time, if you can, every morning and evening for that purpose?

(2) At each time, if you have leisure, to read a chapter out of the Old and one out of the New Testament; if you cannot do this, to take a single chapter, or a part of one?

(3) To read this with a single eye, to know the whole will of God, and a fixed resolution to do it?

In order to know His will, you should,

(4) Have a constant eye to the analogy of faith, the connexion and harmony there is between those grand, fundamental doctrines, original sin, justification by faith, the new birth, inward and outward holiness;

(5) Serious and earnest prayer should be constantly used before we consult the oracles of God; seeing 'Scripture can only be understood through the same Spirit whereby it was given.' Our reading should likewise be closed with prayer, that what we read may be written on our hearts;

*(6) It might also be of use, if, while we read, we were fre-
quently to pause, and examine ourselves by what we read,
both with regard to our hearts and lives....*

*And whatever light you then receive should be used to
the uttermost, and that immediately. Let there be no delay.
Whatever you resolve begin to execute the first moment you
can. So shall you find this word to be indeed the power of
God unto present and eternal salvation.*

These historic leaders were not talking about Bible
study as a mechanical obligation, but as a life-giving
pattern of our lives. History was shaped from this kind
of conviction and commitment.

Bible Study Tools

There is a wealth of Bible study tools available for everyone, for any believer and Bible-reader, to the teacher, or pastor, or scholar. Every year there are new or updated resources.

To see a list and links to some of these high quality Bible study tools, go to:

www.WordWay.org/HowToStudyTheBible

Under "Resources" and "Bible study tools" you will find information about some of the latest study Bibles, Bible dictionaries, encyclopedias, commentaries, and more.

You will also find information about how to use online resources.

A word of caution: it is easy to find websites that have comments on the Bible and interpretations. Many of them are poor quality and have unreliable information. You want to know that any Bible study help you use is based on good scholarship, and is up to date.

For more resources, including downloadable group discussion guide...

www.WordWay.org/HowToStudyTheBible

Do you ever wish you understood the Bible better?

Almost everyone does. Mature believers and new believers. Young and old. Those who have read the Bible for years and those just starting out.

How to Understand the Bible: A Simple Guide, will help you gain an overall perspective on the flow and meaning of Scripture. It addresses questions like: What is the big picture of the Bible? What about Bible translations? How should we understand the stories of the Old Testament? How should we interpret what the prophets had to say? How should we understand the teachings of Jesus? What was Jesus teaching in the parables? How can we hear God's voice in Scripture? What are the proper ways to apply Scripture to life today? Available at amazon.com.

WWW.WORDWAY.ORG